EMPATH
And NARCISSIST

A **Survival Guide** for **Highly Sensitive People**.

How to Defend Yourself and Heal from *Narcissistic Abuse*, *Toxic Codependency*, and *Manipulation* to Become **the Master of Your Emotions**

MICHELLE LUNA BRIGHT

Also by *Michelle Bright*

Copyright © 2022 **Michelle Luna Bright**

All rights reserved. No part of this publication may be reproduced, stored in a retrieval system or transmitted in any form or by any means, electronic, mechanical, photocopying or otherwise, without the prior written permission of the publisher, except in the case of brief quotations embodied in critical reviews and certain other non commercial uses permitted by copyright law.

TABLE *of* CONTENTS

Introduction 6

The Highly Sensitive World of an Empath: Who Is an Empath? 8
- ❖ *Character Traits of an Empath* 11

Different Types of Empaths, Archetypes 15
- ❖ *Useful Empaths Abilities* 20
- ❖ *The Downside of Being an Empath* 23

Understanding Your Empathic Nature 25

The Narcissist: An Identikit of a Toxic Manipulator 30
- ❖ *What are the Traits of a Narcissist?* 30

The Signs You Are in a Narcissist Relationship 40
- ❖ *Why We Attract Narcissists?* 44

A Narcissist Weakness Points 48

Relationships with a Narcissist 52
- ❖ *Different Types of Abusive Behavior* 52
- ❖ *What Is Emotional Abuse?* 57

The Dark Empath 65

Defeat Your Fear 70
- ❖ *What Are Boundaries?* 86

- ❖ *3 Rules to Be Happy as an Empath* 89
- ❖ *The Seven Stages to Create Your Shield* 91

Codependent No More: Your New Life 99

Give Yourself Time to Heal 108

Master Your Emotion and Your Thought Process 112

Improve – 5 Elements of Emotional Intelligence 113
- ❖ *How to Master and Control Anger* 114

Practice 4-steps Meditation – Anger Management 118
- ❖ *How to Master and Control Anxiety* 118
- ❖ *How to Master and Control Depression* 119

Be Successful 123

Set Objective and Attainable Goals 136

Can an Empath Be Extroverted? 139

Always Learn New Skills! 141

The Therapy Option 143

Sustaining Your Relationship Through the Gift of Empathy 146

Introduction

If you're reading this book, you are a great, powerful, and full-of-resources creature! This book will help you in your relationship or even save someone that you know is struggling with empath and narcissistic abuse. If you are in a relationship with someone who seeks attention and admiration but doesn't consider your needs or feelings, you may be dealing with a narcissist. Today, the term may be misunderstood as strong self-love, but that is not the case. It's a behavior incompatible with a functioning society and in contrast to other human beings.

A narcissist is an individual who shows extreme, often unconscious, admiration for himself in an idealized or grandiose way, with the only goal of inflating their over-developed ego. Narcissists are often described as selfish, manipulative, and demanding because they take pleasure to place a lot of attention on themselves at the expense of those they should love and care about.

In psychology, the generic word "narcissism" is often viewed as a disorder called *Narcissistic Personality Disorder* which portrays the individual as a person lacking empathy and consideration for the emotions and well-being of others.

Friendships, relationships, family life, and every other connection the narcissist has with others are always profoundly affected. Most disturbing is the fact that people with such behavioral traits are resistant to change even when it becomes evident that such behavior is causing tension with others.

Nothing's ever the narcissist's fault. He passively blames other people, the world, luck, the weather... anything but himself; they usually preach responsibility, but they are never really able to carry it on their shoulders, as they are not capable of looking within themselves and seeing the problem for what it really is: they are self-absorbed!

People with narcissistic tendencies are also extremely sensitive; feigning a superior stance, they tend to react badly to criticism, disagreement, and comments because they consider personal attacks.

The truth is, life is not exciting for narcissists because they are the king of their world, and when you're king, the dim reality surrounding you (life problems, challenges, hiccups) can show the king naked, and that hurts. The bubble could burst, and the grandiosity of their fantasies fade. Their idea of the world is smeared by fantasies of success, brilliance, and power, and whatever opinion may contradict this delusion is either ignored or fought off entirely.

Remember, a narcissist is weak. But if you are one of those unique highly sensitive people, you are a strength that you may have never realized yet. Not only can you handle him, but you can be victorious with a smile on your face.

Your relationship may be significant to you, but if you are always near a narcissist, you may want to start analyzing your life choices. You will discover that a relationship with a narcissist can impact your mental health.

The first thing you need to do then is to raise up your defenses. But before you get there, you should know yourself and your potential.

AN EMPATHIC INDIVIDUAL

The most striking features of an empathic person are her feelings and the ability to absorb the emotions of others. It is possible that there were times you felt like someone else was taking advantage of you because of your nature, but this unique trait you have is really exceptional.

If you paid close attention to the above details describing a narcissist, you would agree that everything mentioned is in sharp contrast with your personality. Empathic people are highly sensitive, in a good way, which makes it possible for them to think beyond themselves when faced with a situation that involves others.

I'm going to take you through a journey that will hopefully help you understand a lot about yourself and the people that may affect you. I've been there myself, and I'm living proof that life can change.

May you be bold, strong, and full of hope. And remember, a smile can kill a demon.

The Highly Sensitive World of an Empath:

Who Is an Empath?

Empaths are mindful, kind, superiorly sensitive individuals who often feel the vocation to help others. They are frequently found being involved in action of charity or kindness, they represent the Guardian Angel archetype and feel the duty to serve others—sometimes too much —and it's not rare to see them working as childcare suppliers, medicinal experts, hospice laborers, birthing specialists, and such. Most empaths came into the world with the untold mission to mend humans, creatures, plants, and the planet. They are natural healers, they absorb so much outside and other people's vitality that they must invest a large portion of their time to clear unwanted energy, and to get into a cleanse state to steam pressure off.

Here are a couple of attributes of empaths who have not figured out how to sift through other individuals' feelings or deal with their very own vitality:

- You always feel overpowered with feelings, and you may cry a great deal, feel pitiful, furious, or discouraged without any justifiable cause. You might be enticed to think you are insane for having arbitrary emotional episodes and episodes of unexplained weakness. On the off chance that you are a lady, it resembles always having PMS! Intemperate sympathy can make individuals show symptoms like bipolar (hyper burdensome) disorder.

- You drop by the store feeling incredible, yet once you get in a group, you start feeling down, furious, miserable or overpowered. In an ailment-like state, you choose to return home and rest.

- You discover that you can't open up without getting overpowered, you may decide to carry on with the life of a loner. However, even at home, you get discouraged when you watch the news and cry while watching a movie. You feel terrible when business for the Humane Society brings to your attention creatures that need a home. You want to save a more significant number of animals than you can think about.

- You feel frustrated about individuals regardless of what their identity is or what they have done. You want to stop and help anybody in your way. You can't go by a homeless without giving him cash, regardless of whether you don't have it to save.

- Many empaths are overweight. When they assimilate unpleasant feelings, it can trigger fits of anxiety, despair just as food, sex, and useless medication are consumed. Some may indulge in adapting to passionate pressure or utilize their body weight as a shield to hide behind.

- Most empaths can act as human sponges by absorbing others' pains by drawing the agony or sickness out of the wiped-out individual and into their bodies. For apparent reasons, this isn't suggested except if you realize how to keep from winding up sick as you walk through other's dark caves.

- You suffer from physical symptoms like chest pain, stomach spasms, headaches or fever without being specifically ill. You then discover in hindsight that your "disease" matched with the beginning of a companion's or relative's sickness.

- It's very difficult to mislead you since you can see through their facade and into people's souls. More often than not, you just know what they are thinking.

- People—even outsiders—open up and start telling you their stuff. You might sit in the lounge area minding your own business, even trying to avoid human contact, when the individual next to you starts sharing a wide range of personal information. You didn't ask them to, and they never thought that you might not have any desire to absorb their life drama. People usually feel better after having shared with you, yet you wind up feeling worse because they have moved their passionate torment into you.

- Some empaths don't do well with close connections. Always taking on their partner's agony and feelings, they may effortlessly get their feelings hurt, want to spend time alone instead of with the partner, feel defenseless when engaging in sexual relations, and think that they need to ceaselessly recover their vitality when it gets cluttered with that of their partner. They might be so terrified to be overwhelmed by someone else that they close up just to survive.

- The sick, the afflicted, and the oppressed are attracted to the unrestricted comprehension and empathy an empath emanates without limit. Until you figure out a way to turn away other people's bad influence, you might live in an upsetting reality where the only way to survive is to isolate yourself.

It's anything but difficult to perceive any reason why being an empath is frequently extremely tiring. It's no big surprise that a few people shut down their empathic capacity after some time. What's more, with that, they likewise shut down an essential piece of their celestial direction framework. Determine how to deal with the amount of information you receive and select only what is extremely significant.

❖ Character Traits Of An Empath

Being an empath means that, on the one hand, you are influenced by other individuals' energies while, on the other hand, you have a natural capacity to feel and see others instinctively. Empaths can see others' physical sensitivities and profound inclinations, inspirations, and goals. You either are an empath, or you aren't, you can't become one. You are always open to processing other individuals' sentiments and vitality, which implies that you truly feel, and, by and large, assume the feelings of others. Many empaths experience things like constant weakness, ecological sensitivities, or unexplained unease daily. All these elements impact your persona from the outside. Basically, you are strolling around in this world with the majority of the collected karma, feelings, and vitality taken from others.

If you still have doubts about whether or not you can call yourself an empath, read these character qualities and try to look at yourself with an outsider's eyes. This rundown will also be useful when attempting to understand if someone you know is an empath too.

1. Profoundly Delicate

Generally, an empathic individual is the most sensitive in the room and rapidly gets even the smallest changes in others. They can "feel into" other individuals and can profoundly comprehend their feelings, inspirations, and sentiments. But their high sensitivity, the natural high extension of their antennas, also make them sensible, the stimuli coming their way are very amplified by their receptors. Their extreme sensibility isn't limited merely to physical sensations—it also incorporates relational angles.

2. Exceptionally Natural

In numerous cases, empaths are profoundly in contact with their sentiments and feelings. They have a much-improved comprehension of their passionate self than many others. That's why empathic individuals should always figure out ways to keep control of their gut impulses; often they are unsuccessful, and instinct takes over. This "natural" way of behaving can often bring awkwardness in their relationships, leading them to evade profoundly harmful and manipulative individuals. Again, unfortunately, this is not always the case.

3. Exceptionally Thoughtful

Just because somebody is contemplative, it doesn't mean they are an empath, and also the other way around is true. In fact, not every single empathic individual is inherently thoughtful. For most, though, they tend to feel more balanced in an environment that encompasses few individuals. Even if they can feel good around energetic and kind companions, they rapidly feel overpowered when these people come in groups, making them want to escape the gatherings. Therefore, they regularly prefer to use their energy alone or in a context with few social associations because they feel it will enhance their intrinsic capacities.

4. Selfless

While narcissists just consider themselves, empaths frequently will, in general, overlook their very own needs. Much of the time, they are so worried about the prosperity of others that they thoroughly neglect to deal with their own. Empaths may even turn out to be so drenched in a compassionate venture that they dismiss everything else, regardless of whether it causes them extraordinary future challenges.

5. Interfaces with Others (as Well) Rapidly

When empathic individuals feel a safe bond, they can build strong relationships with others quite quickly. They may associate with those special individuals on such a personal and profound level and in such a brief period that others will most likely be unable to keep their pace. Therefore, these individuals may feel as though the empath is excessively rapid in getting personal, which may feel unnatural to them.

6. Excessively Soft, Sometimes

Empaths regularly see themselves in others. Thus, they can quickly put themselves in others' shoes and understand what their issues are. They are very mindful of how the psychological weight that a few people carry on their shoulders impacts their conduct. Hence, they are now and again excessively lenient with other individuals' unsatisfactory and rude behavior. Rather than not enabling others to treat them unfairly, empaths are probably going to rationalize other individuals' behavior.

7. The Inclination to Put Others Before Themselves

Empathic individuals are not just exceptionally caring, they also likewise tend to put others before themselves. They are generally disposed to accept that the requirements of others are unquestionably more important than their one-of-a-kind needs. This angel personality leads those who may abuse them to keep them nearby.

8. Finds Falsehoods and Duplicities Incredibly Quick

From numerous points of view, empaths seem to have the extraordinary capacity to see through other people's lies and manipulation rapidly. They might be exceptionally suspicious of fake individuals, while a large number of their peers haven't seen a thing.

9. Intrinsic Want to Better the World

Many profoundly empathic individuals' activities are driven by their desire to improve the world. They invest significantly more energy with exercises of a helpful or kind nature than in progressively egotistical ventures. They see the bigger picture whereas others only see their personal gain.

10. Curious In Nature

Another character quality of empaths is their curiosity. They are rarely happy with the convictions of others, no matter how they try to convince them. Even if they tend to accept others' opinions, under the surface, they will need their own proof. Hence, they consistently attempt to perceive what is held behind the curtain. This is because of their curious nature, but not only are they continually looking for answers, they also love to suggest their own interesting ideas, which sometimes can cause them to lose themselves in fantasies and ethereal philosophies.

11. Obliviousness

Empaths are regularly seen to be oblivious, absent-minded, or heedless. In actuality, empathic individuals are so overwhelmed by the ocean of feelings they are swimming in, that they risk to drown. They are taken away by the confusing feelings they are shrouded with, which regularly drives them to turn out to be completely drenched in their musings and opinions.

12. Readiness to Acknowledge Full Responsibility

The average person constantly blames others for their lack. An empathic person is the opposite. Rather than looking for external causes, empaths tend to assume full responsibility for their behavior right away. This may sound like a good quality, but more often than not, they may acknowledge the responsibility for things they are not in any manner accountable for.

13. Exceptionally Inventive

An empathic individual is (as a rule) exceptionally imaginative. They want to invest their energy in exercises that enable them to utilize their creative mind and inventiveness. Empaths' souls are bound to be craftsmen, scholars, artists, painters, and fashioners rather than bookkeepers, legal counselors, and architects.

Different Types of Empaths, *Archetypes*

The empath is a general category within which we can identify six specifications depending on how you relate to your gift and the ways it manifests most strongly for you. For some, the energy comes through emotions and feelings, while for others, it emerges as having a keen sensitivity to plants and animals instead of people.

Usually, even if you are one of these kinds of Empath, you may show gifts in one of the other categories too. Now, what kind of Empath are you?

EMOTIONAL EMPATH

An emotional Empath is exactly what it sounds like: someone who strongly senses and feels the emotions of another. It is not an easy thing to deal with in your life, especially if you are not aware you are an Empath yet, and you are dealing with a lot of other people's baggage and not just your own.

It is a highly prevalent form of empathy and will usually be linked to other types. It comes with the need to have a lot of alone time and opportunities to recharge your batteries after the exhaustion of feeling so many different people's emotional energy.

You can determine if you are an emotional Empath if you are always giving a lot of your time to other people and working hard to solve their emotional problems to the point of exhaustion. People will often naturally and unconsciously cling to an emotional Empath because of how good they are at listening and how they often make people feel better.

An emotional empath absorbs the negative feelings of another like a sponge, lifting the worries, fears, and doubts of the friend in need but then taking that energy away with them, like a garbage collector.

Emotional Empaths need a lot of focused energy clearing, grounding, and personal honesty with their feelings and emotions to live in a healthy balance with their gifts. True emotional Empaths will also want to look for friends and partnerships that allow them to have a more balanced emotional life. Emotional empaths often get involved in very toxic relationships because they are always acting as a caregiver to their partner's emotional needs and are rarely or infrequently given the same in return leading to deficient energy and several negative and unhealthy negative side-effects.

PHYSICAL EMPATH

Physical empaths are usually emotional empaths who can also perceive physical pain from another person. It is often a way for you to assess how someone feels on the physical level and is not as common as emotional empathy. If you are a physical Empath, you would know it. You would feel the pain of the person sitting next to you or take home someone's raging headache.

Have you ever heard the term "sympathy pain"? It is a real thing that can occur for any person and will often result in taking on someone's physical feelings in an empathic way. Some men have claimed to feel the labor pains of childbirth while their partners give birth to their babies. It is an example of what physical empathy might feel.

However, for the physical empath, the experiences are much more frequent and involve even the subtlest vibration of physical discomfort. It can also relate to pleasure and joy, including sexual feelings or orgasmic moments that are felt or shared in partnership.

There are various ways this "feeling" will manifest for the physical empath, and it is essential to make sure that whatever you are feeling belongs to you and not to someone else, similar to emotional empaths requiring boundaries with people's sensitive feelings. Some hypochondriacs might just be physical/emotional Empaths who haven't identified their gifts yet.

PLANT EMPATH

People who are plant Empaths are those who are deeply connected to the energy of living things that are not human. A plant Empath can often "hear" what a plant or living organism might need or even understand the language that they speak. Accustomed plant empaths can feel a cathartic release in writing down nature's feelings. Plant Empaths are excellent at perceiving the power of plants and the energy they bring into the world.

A green thumb is undoubtedly a component of being empathic with plants, and many people who are naturally gifted gardeners will possess varying levels and degrees of plant empathy. The best way to understand plant empathy is to consider how you feel when you are around them. Many plants are very high in vibration, meaning they have very light and pure energy. Being around them makes most people feel good, and for someone with strong plant empath skills, it will be a much stronger sensation of joy and happiness.

To become a plant empath, all you need is to study how they want to communicate. Many people will read endless books about the proper way to garden or remove pests and bugs from the leaves and soil, but these are all very human concepts. What about asking the plant what it "thinks"? For the plant Empath, this wouldn't be strange at all, and if you consider that they are living beings, also you wouldn't hesitate to inquire what their needs are daily, just as you would a person or even an animal, which brings us to the next type of empath.

ANIMAL EMPATH

As you may have imagined from the name, an animal Empath can sense the feelings of animals. It doesn't just mean pets or domesticated animals; it can also mean a flock, a herd, or a colony. Being an animal empath will often coincide with being an emotional Empath and sensing people's feelings, but for those who are especially sensitive to human emotions, the warmth of cats and dogs can be a little bit easier to manage on a day-to-day level.

Some animal Empaths spend their careers working with a variety of pets or species of animals through veterinary and rescue services, while others will just live with a lot of pets and rescue animals at their homes, living in harmony with all of the animals they meet.

You don't have to be an animal empath to appreciate animals, but it is an animal Empath who can perceive the needs, feelings, and pain of an animal which comes in handy considering that animals cannot speak English to describe what they are going through. Animal empaths pick up on those needs and can help animals through a higher sensitivity as they "read" the animal's energy and intention.

Animal empaths are a lot like people empaths in the way they read the energy of another, and it can be through this gift that you can find your most fulfilling career and living situation in close company with a variety of unique animal friends.

ENVIRONMENTAL EMPATH

Environmental empathy has a much larger scale. For those who are environmental empaths, they will sense the "feelings" of an entire landscape. Imagine a mountainside wholly shorn of all of its trees destined for a lumber yard. Think of all of the forest's inhabitants that were uprooted and killed so the trees could be cut.

It is what environmental empaths will sense: the pain of the land that has experienced destruction. They can feel the peacefulness and harmony of the nation as well, and some empaths will choose their home based on the way the landscape and environment feel.

Environmental empaths are also capable of sensing places, not just natural landscapes. They might walk into an old building that has seen a long and violent history, noticing the energy of how hundreds of years of religious torment left many vibrations and feelings behind in the walls and floors.

When an environmental empath walks into a building built on the protected and sacred land of an indigenous people without permission, they can feel the intense energy of deceit, deception, and wrongdoing. They can also contact the vibration and frequency of goodness, compassion, and sympathy in the walls of a particular structure, which could come from the way it is built, or the business inside of it.

Environmental empaths are often activists for the Earth and its resplendent beauty, as well as for peoples and places that need a voice to celebrate them or avoid destruction and disharmony. It is often the job of the environmental empath to help protect the natural world and create consciousness around the way we live on Earth.

INTUITIVE EMPATH

Intuitive Empaths are really near to a psychic. In a way, they are telepathic and can have a powerful sense of things to come. They are also gifted emotional Empaths and may even have all of the other empathic gifts listed above, but the main contribution is an ability to have clairvoyance and psychic perception.

Those gifts wake up in those empaths who are allowed to explore this side of their persona early in life, or by a personal spiritual journey that ignites the ability to see the world in this new way. When we are young, the way we see the world depends on what we are told and how we're programmed; an early age-restricted mindset can very well engage these gifts, and we may not know about our true nature until it comes knocking on our door.

Many people find their psychic awareness later on in life through their own choices and ability to grow in that direction. Intuitive Empaths very often begin their journeys as emotional Empaths as their inherent skills widen and intensify over time and with experience.

Intuitive Empaths are good at predicting a moment or situation before it happens and can also assess or pinpoint deeper meanings behind the emotional pain of another. They are also often able to see the past lives of another person and even have prophetic dreams and visions that shed light on important matters in their own lives and those around them.

Psychics will not always describe themselves as intuitive empaths, but that is basically what they are. They can read beyond the layer of emotion and see the energy of all possibilities for anyone or anything in the world. It takes a lot of practice and personal growth to achieve this type of empathy, but every emotional empath can do it if they are very inclined to walk that path.

All of these types of empaths illustrate the reality of what being an empath means. Feeling empathic towards someone you know or a situation you are in is one thing; sensing, touching, perceiving, and absorbing those feelings is quite another matter. Consider what types of empaths you are and begin to see the correlation to your life experiences as they are right now.

Finding your type is what will help you identify the best ways to take control of your gift. You may be wondering at this point if being an Empath is a good thing. Wouldn't life be better if it wasn't so complicated and sensitive? It may be. But being gifted always brings many blessings.

❖ Useful Empaths Abilities

Psychic Abilities

Some empaths may develop psychic abilities. Environmental, physical/medical, animal, plant, and intuitive empaths all possess psychic abilities to some degree if they dig deep enough. This special type of ability goes beyond just sensing what those around an empath are going through. Empaths with psychic abilities can often sense what is going to happen to someone despite being miles away from them. They will often be hit suddenly with a flood of sensations that alerts them about what is happening far away even though they are nowhere near this person. An empath's heightened senses and high levels of empathy can result in them developing psychic abilities or a sixth sense. Empaths who go on to develop their empath gift may find that their psychic abilities come out more clearly. A second manuscript will be dedicated specifically to this topic, but as for now, let's see some of these abilities.

Visions

The heightened senses of an empath allow them to look at things from a different perspective. They can focus on the finer details of a situation or person to truly understand what is happening around them and in the other person's life. This ability allows them to tune out the other noise to find a deeper meaning and find the key factors that need one's attention. Not all empaths can develop this ability to its fullest, yet if an empath does develop this ability but lacks the understanding of how to utilize it properly, they may put themselves at great risk of being taken advantage of.

Intuition

Everybody already has some level of intuition, but an empath has a stronger intuition, or I should call it awareness. When empaths come to a strong sense of self, they can develop their intuitive abilities fully. While intuitive empaths naturally have this ability, other empaths can tap into their intuition as well at a slower pace. This intuition can help guide them in navigating their social realities and allows them to better address certain situations. With this ability, empaths can diffuse negative situations before they occur, allowing them to have better judgments about people.

An empath's intuition is seldom wrong. Only when an empath lacks self-respect and trust in herself will her intuition be off. For this reason, an empath needs to gain a better understanding of themselves, all their abilities, and unique qualities to better use their intuitive powers.

Telepathy

This is an ability that only a few empaths can develop. Telepathic abilities allow empaths to understand another person's thoughts fully and to communicate in alternative means of communication their own intentions. For those who get naturally to this stage, it's easy to know exactly where emotional responses are coming from. An empath may use this ability to further help other people heal and recognize their own thought patterns that cause them to have negative or positive emotional responses.

Natural Healing

An empath's ability to connect with others makes them a natural healer. Because so many individuals seem just to be drawn to empaths and feel more comfortable around them, empaths can really listen and understand what an individual needs to fix. Physical empaths are the aptest to heal individuals on a different level by sharing what changes one would need to make to recover from an illness or health condition. That said, all empaths can do this to some degree.

Seeing Through Lies

Empaths who learn to seep away the noise of misdirecting communication can work as lie detectors. They can easily understand when someone is dishonest. Whether the words you say are a lie or the way you present yourself to others is covering who you truly are, an empath knows you're lying. Some can even identify what you are lying about. This lead empaths to avoid people they know to be dishonest as these people tend to give off negative energies and, therefore, can leave an empath feeling ill or extremely fatigued.

Heightened Senses

Empaths are easily overstimulated due to their heightened senses. This is why an empath prefers to choose calmer and quieter environments. Bright colors, lights, and noise can increase the anxiety that an empath is already prone to feel. This heightened sensitivity to external objects can often add to the overwhelming feeling that empaths struggle to cope with when they are in large crowds. It is also why they tend to be very careful about where they work, as many work environments can trigger these senses, making it impossible for them to be productive.

Creativity

Most empaths have highly creative talents. They tend to look at things from a unique perspective more easily and can be incredibly innovative. For this reason, empaths with good training can also make incredibly successful entrepreneurs. Music, art, and other creative outlets that let an empath be hands-on are things they are likely to thrive at.

Most empaths find themselves in some sort of creative industry. This is because of their ability to look at things differently, think of innovative ideas, and have a deeper sense of being able to understand what is possible—meaning they can take simple ideas (their own or in collaboration with others) and turn those ideas into something tangible. Empaths are dreamers, but they do not just simply dream; they quietly set out to make their dreams a reality.

❖ The Downside Of Being An Empath

Green empaths can be easily manipulated, especially by those who are aware of their soft spots. When a toxic personality, like a narcissist, identifies an empath, they will try to take advantage of them by taking control, little by little, of their destiny. Empaths naturally attract others, and negative people are often more attracted to an empath than positive ones. The caring and giving nature of an empath, keeps them on constant guard. While they trust their intuition, and many of them can often spot these negative or toxic people, this doesn't put a hold on the deep desire of wanting to help them.

This, plus the fact that many empaths tend to feel incredibly insecure about themselves., is a recipe for unhappiness. The insecurity is brought on not just because of the energy they absorb but because their abilities are often misunderstood. They often feel like outsiders and will try to hide what they are capable of to fit in. Empaths are also people pleasers. This deep desire to help everyone they come in contact with can lead to them having a victim mentality or being codependent.

Empaths need their "alone time" and often tend to retreat or hide in it. They have a hard time battling with this facade they put on in front of everyone else while knowing deep in their nature they were born to help others. This is where an empath enters in a conflicting stage. It is a stage where many ignore their abilities and settle for a life they are never really comfortable with. On the other hand, some learn to embrace their abilities and take the first step to embrace who they are and what they feel, making a clearer understanding of their being and their purpose.

Now you should have an idea of which empath you are. Is your increased awareness directed especially to people, or can you also feel the energy of other living things like animals and plants? Knowing what kind of empath you are will help develop those specific abilities that come with that type of empath. You may also have understood that there are possibilities ahead of you that you haven't accessed yet.

Understanding Your Empathic Nature

Your journey toward identifying your empathic nature starts with self-awareness and being able to identify the unique characteristics that make you who you are. While we can all display different behaviors depending on the situation, it's easy to identify the patterns of behavior that we routinely engage in.

It's important to remember that most people, empaths or otherwise, have a natural level of empathy and consideration for others. Empaths are set apart by their higher sensitivity and ability to not just understand but also feel other people's emotions. If you can see yourself in one of the following categories, you can safely say you are an empath and to what extent.

You Are a Great Listener

Empaths are known to be incredible listeners. In fact, many tend to be the "counselor" in their friend group. You may notice that your friends, family, loved ones, and maybe even complete strangers come to you with their problems and want to talk. At times, it may also feel like you are an emotional dumping ground for people's thoughts and emotions.

As an Empath, you have a strong ability to listen to others and truly feel what they are sharing with you. They especially like talking to you because people feel like you hear what they aren't saying and know the problem better than they do, which can be a great relief for many. Modern society is not overly accepting of many thoughts, feelings, or emotions. As a result, many people are uncomfortable or seemingly incapable of sharing these things because you seem to "just know" people may be drawn to you. After all, it feels like a breath of fresh air being understood in ways that no one has likely ever understood them before.

You May Struggle to Connect to Standard Religion

Many Empaths find it extremely challenging to connect to the teachings of most modern religions. Although most Empaths will see and appreciate the underlying messages of connection and unconditional love, they tend to pick up on the reality that most religious organizations do not actually live or operate in alignment with these teachings. This can lead to a deep inner sense of struggle for any Empaths who have been raised in or around a religious community. They want to see the good in it all and connect with their loved ones, but many see right through the teachings and find themselves feeling frustrated with the deception that seems to go on with many religious groups. Furthermore, Empaths highly value freedom and free will, both of which are rarely honored in spiritual teachings. For this reason, most empaths will find themselves being heavily drawn away from religious teachings, perhaps even growing a deep sense of resentment toward them and all that they stand for.

You Are Drawn to Spirituality

Despite not being attracted to religious teachings, many empaths will be attracted to spirituality. Spirituality tends to be more accepting of and understanding toward Empaths, allowing them to feel understood and recognized by others. This also facilitates deep connections between the teachings and those who follow similar paths. This type of connection can be heavily empowering for Empaths, allowing them to feel supported in their journey as they also support others. Since the spiritual path is filled with Empaths, many Empaths trust that the individuals in these journeys will think similarly to them and, therefore, will be more accepting, understanding, empathetic, compassionate, and caring towards them. This allows them to feel reciprocated, making it far more inviting than many standard religious teachings.

In addition to supporting them in feeling understood, many spirituality-based teachings actually elaborate on the meaning of being an Empath and support Empaths in understanding themselves and refining their talents. This means that through these teachings, the empath can further their own sense of self-understanding and work more passionately alongside their life and spiritual purposes with clear direction, guidance, and support.

You Struggle to Keep Healthy Boundaries

One symptom many Empaths face is struggling to keep healthy boundaries. Because an Empath can sense exactly what another person is feeling or experiencing, they may find themselves regularly making excuses for the other person. Things such as "oh, they didn't mean to" or "they only did this because deep down they are hurting" regularly come to mind. Although these deep understandings of others can be valuable, they can also result in the empath being taken advantage of and used by others with less empathy or none.

The difficulty of maintaining healthy boundaries, or any limitations at all, for empaths, can be a major point of trauma. Because empath strives to see the good in others, they may let people repeatedly take advantage of them or abuse them because they struggle to connect to the reality that you cannot help someone who does not want to help themselves. You may feel like you have to be the "savior," even though the chances of this panning out are extremely slim.

You May Struggle with Addictions

Empaths are known to struggle with addictions. Many use addictions as a coping method to attempt to "shut off" their empathy or numb them toward the world around them. While this may seem to work, the reality is that nothing can actually shut off their gift. Instead, what often ends up happening is that they begin to dissociate from their feelings and ignore the reality of their empathic abilities. Over time, this leads to a deep sense of depression because they take on an excessive amount of energy and emotion, create even more within themselves, and never effectively deal with or release any of these energies or emotions.

Addictions within Empaths are not restricted to substance abuse. They may also be drawn to overeating, oversleeping, or never sleeping to avoid nightmares and restlessness, video games, or otherwise obsessively attempting to draw their attention away from reality to avoid the pain they are experiencing suffering with.

You Are Likely Highly Creative

Empathic individuals are almost always highly creative. They perceive the world differently and tend to see art where others see virtually nothing. For example, an Empath may look at a blank page and see an entire image come to life, thus drawing them into wanting to create that image and bring it into reality. Empaths have visual gifts unlike any other, allowing them to quite literally think things into existence. An individual who is not empathic would likely see just a blank page. Empaths are known to become artists on varying levels. They may create art through words, objects, perception, photography, or virtually anything else. The entire world is a canvas to empaths and they just want to create. Creating allows them to express themselves in ways that words and emotions do not always allow for. Additionally, it allows them to feel incredible self-worth, empowered and inspired by the world around them.

You Can "Feel" Others

Empathic people can "feel" others. As you may have picked up, this is actually one of the first things that identify an Empath. If you can feel others either emotionally, mentally, or physically, or any combination of these three, there is a good chance that you are an Empath. These symptoms allow you to step into the reality of others and experience what they are experiencing in a way that the average person cannot.

When it comes to empathy, ordinary people experiencing empathy can relate what someone else is experiencing to something that they have experienced themselves in the past. However, for an Empath, it is much deeper than that. You do not relate people to your own experiences. Instead, you directly feel theirs. This is what allows Empaths to feel things that they have never personally experienced before. For example, if someone were to tell you that they had a concussion, you may feel the exact symptoms they are experiencing, even if you have never had a concussion before.

You May Have Suffered from Narcissistic Abuse

Narcissists are drawn to Empaths because they have the one thing that the narcissist completely lacks: empathy. Empaths, as you know, have a heightened level of empathy that is above average. This makes them more desirable than the average person because they have enough to substitute for the lack of empathy that the narcissist has. Furthermore, Empaths are more likely to forgive and desire to see the good in other people. This means that it is easy for a narcissist to draw Empaths into their abuse cycles and quickly turn their empathic gift into a burden that they long to destroy so that they can step away.

You May Feel Extremely Close to Plants and Animals

Empaths, especially plant Empaths and animal Empaths, tend to feel extremely close to plants and animals. Even if you are not a plant or animal Empath, you may still find yourself feeling extremely drawn to them. This is because they tend to have much purer energy, filled with unconditional love. For many Empaths, plants and animals are a breath of fresh air from the corrupted society that many of us live in.

If you find that you are heavily drawn to plants and animals, and especially if you feel like you can communicate with them in a paranormal way, this may be an indication that you are experiencing your empathic gifts. The unconditional love you feel between each other is simply amazing and blissful. You may even think that your plants and pets are the only things that can make you feel better when things are not going well. If you feel that you receive wisdom and advice from plants and animals, this is your claircognizant gift arising from your empathic abilities.

You Might Have Experienced Mental or Physical Symptoms

Empaths often experience mental and physical symptoms relating to their gift and the more commonly talked about emotional symptoms. These are not always directly borrowed from someone else but may actually be the symptom of feeling so many other people's energies so deeply. Many Empaths may experience psychotic attacks or episodes because they feel overwhelmed by the amount of energy around them that they are always picking up. Empaths often feel like they are a "sponge" to the world around them, which can result in them picking up and holding on too many different sensations.

Some of the common mental or physical symptoms you are likely to face are those that are related to experiencing chronic high stress. The body can only carry so many different energies and emotions before it becomes too much for it. Then, it begins to maximize its output of cortisol, the stress hormone, causing you to start experiencing emotional, mental, and physical symptoms related to personal stress. This could be anything from physical pain to anxiety and depression, and even recurring thoughts based on suicide or self-harm. It is important to understand that these symptoms are often concerning your empathic gift. They are generally heightened by experiencing other people's stress and the stress from feeling these feelings without properly managing them within yourself. In other words, you are not stepping out, so the stress is getting blocked within you.

The Narcissist: *An Identikit of a Toxic Manipulator*

WHO IS A NARCISSIST?

If you ask someone who a narcissist is, most people will describe an arrogant, entitled, privileged male. This is the person that has been promoted as a "narcissist" in most people's lives. However, the reality is that narcissists are not quite as defined as that. A narcissist can truly be anyone. There is no preferred gender, age, or race that narcissism chooses. Instead, anyone can be a narcissist.

In the United States, it is estimated that 1 in every 25 people is a sociopath. Sociopaths are those who are at the top end of the spectrum that also contains psychopaths and narcissists. The number of narcissistic individuals living in modern America is surprisingly large. The majority of us come across at least one in our lives that impacts us in some way. For some of us, that impact is significant. For others, recognize the behavior to be negative and walk away.

Rather than looking at the demographics of "who" a narcissist is, it is easier to identify one by their traits. A narcissist's list of characteristics that identify their narcissistic behaviors is reasonably straightforward and is the easiest way to determine a narcissist. Attempting to use statistical evidence around their demographic will not result in an accurate finding.

❖ What Are The Traits Of A Narcissist?

Paying attention to the traits of an individual is the easiest way to identify whether or not someone is a narcissist. If you want to identify one, pay attention to the list of traits below and take a moment to consider if the person you are questioning possesses these traits. This will support you in understanding if they truly are a narcissist.

People with narcissistic personality disorder possess these traits:

A Complete Lack of Empathy

First and foremost, narcissistic people possess a complete lack of empathy. Those with a narcissistic personality disorder do not simply lack empathy; they are mentally incapable of experiencing it. This results in them being incapable of identifying the emotions or feelings of others and taking them into account.

Due to a lack of empathy, narcissistic people will struggle to behave in a way that shows no compassion toward other humans. They are incapable of understanding how their actions impact others, and as a result, they are known to behave regularly in a way that is mentally damaging to others. This is how they build on their abuse without showing any signs of feeling remorseful for it: because they truly cannot feel remorse. It can be very toxic and draining to be around someone who has no sign of empathy or takes responsibility for their actions.

Grandiose Sense of Self-Importance

Narcissistic people are known to have an elated sense of self-importance. They will often lie about their achievements to make them sound better than they are. They also lie about their talents so that people will believe they are more capable than they actually are. Narcissist does not just want to be recognized and superior and better, they expect to be. Regardless of their actual achievements, even if they are incredibly few or irrelevant, they expect to be seen as the superior person. No matter what, a narcissist wants to be seen as better than everyone else they meet.

Fantasizes About Unlimited Power or Success

Narcissistic people are obsessed with their fantasies about unlimited power and success. They like to fantasize about being better than everyone else in every way possible, from their looks to their life. They want to be the best at activities, relationships, family, work, and virtually every area of their life. They will do everything they can to make it appear as though they have the best life possible and that it is better than anyone else's. This enables narcissists to have an unrealistic belief of what their life truly is, which often provides a strong basis for how they can deceive other people into believing their fantasy reality versus the actual reality.

Believe They Are "Special"

Narcissistic individuals have a belief that they are "special" in some way. This promotes their inner belief that they are superior to others and why they act so entitled. They believe that they can only be understood by other "special" people, who are typically only those of high status. In fact, many believe they should only associate with people of high status or institutions of high status and often think that they are above everyone else. This belief can be seen in their arrogant behaviors, attitude toward other people, and the way they talk to themselves in groups.

Addicted to Attention

The narcissist's addiction to attention is the driving force behind everything that they do. Narcissists do not just crave attention; they *need* it. This is why they will lie about everything, fantasize about massive success and power, and otherwise focus on things that will earn them some attention, including drama. They may be particularly focused on grooming and maintaining a very poised outward image (their mask or false-self). This is how they can draw in all the attention they crave from other people.

Because of their need for attention, narcissists become abusive. Their carefully crafted abuse cycle enables them to cause other people to become codependent, resulting in these other people not having a sense of self-worth or identity. Then, they are pressured to see this individual as the "godly" aspect of their lives. The codependent will look to the narcissist for validation, approval, and acceptance. The narcissist will offer increments of validation, approval, and acceptance in dosages that become increasingly smaller over time. At first, their withholding of love and kindness only happens every once in a while. Eventually, it happens daily.

Is Envious or Believes Others Are Envious

Narcissists tend to go one or both ways with envy. They either tend to be chronically envious of everyone else, which further drives their need for attention, or they believe that everyone else is envious of them. Most narcissists are both to a degree.

When they are envious of others, the narcissist will rarely say anything. Instead, they will begin to lie and exploit others, even more, to make it appear as though they are not envious and have nothing to be envious about. Remember, a narcissist does not only want to be the best in the room, but they truly believe they *are* at all times. They will say anything they need to say to ensure that everyone else believes this mask and regards them as the best, even if that includes lying, manipulating people, exploiting others, and otherwise being abusive to the people they know and, in many cases, do not know.

When they believe others are envious of them, this feeds into their need for attention. They feel good—like they are winning at their game. They want other people to be envious of them because this is how people feel toward people who are "better." At least, that is what the narcissist believes. The narcissist will say and do anything it takes to ensure they are better than the others, even if they really are not, just so that the other people in the room become envious of them. This supports their need for attention and thus becomes one of their favorite tools for satisfying the addiction.

Arrogant Behavior or Attitude

Despite arrogance itself not being the measure of a narcissist, most narcissists are arrogant. This means that not all arrogant people are narcissists, but all narcissists are arrogant. This arrogant behavior and attitude support them in promoting themselves as the best person in the room. It allows them to portray a higher degree of confidence than they actually possess, allowing them to appear "special" and better than others.

When a narcissist is arrogant, they are the maximum degree of arrogance they can possibly be. They are not just slightly arrogant or walking around with a somewhat inflated ego and sense of self-confidence. People with narcissistic personality disorder take arrogance to the next level. They are extremely inflated in their confidence and ego about absolutely everything. This is a tool they use to appear better, and they use it to the maximum degree.

Compulsive Liars

Narcissists are compulsive liars. As such, they are also experts at manipulating other people. Narcissists will expertly create a web of lies that support them in creating their desired reality and bringing other people into it. If they are ever caught in a lie, they will masterfully create more lies to cover up the lies that they have already told. In this process, they are not worried about who they hurt or who they blame through their lies. Their only concern is in ensuring that they are protected and that they come out looking like the winner in one way or another.

When a narcissist is not outright lying, they will purposefully leave out important pieces of information. Or they will stonewall the victim by refusing to answer any questions or by providing evasive answers to the questions being asked. This is another way of them creating a blameless crime where they can easily spin it around to look like it was someone else's fault for not asking for the information outright, even though they knew that the chances of the other person thinking to asking would be slim. This is how they ensure that even when they are lying, they cannot be blamed for their lies. If anything, you can be blamed for not pressing for more information.

No matter how much you continue digging to discover the full truth or attempt to untangle their lies, you will never get to the real truth. They will continue dancing around the situation until you are so exhausted that you stop. If you do not exhaust before finally reaching their breaking point, you will be so tired from chasing that you can no longer fight or stand up for yourself, thus meaning you are still a victim of the lie even if you finally get to the truth. Either way, the narcissist wins.

Openly Exploits Victims on Social Media

A narcissist has a deep addiction to exploiting their victims. These days, social media has given them the power to exploit, even more, resulting in their victims suffering even further. There are at least five major ways that narcissists will take advantage of social media to exploit you, should they so desire.

The first way is by using social media to enhance further their favorite abuse tool of "triangulation." In essence, they will bring another person into the mixture and embarrass you by giving more attention to the other person than is typically reasonable or acceptable for a relationship. This may lead to you believing they are cheating because they share pictures of them with this other person, or they comment more on their photos than they do on yours, thus making it clearly visible that this other person is getting more attention than you do. Then, when you attempt to point this act out, they will blame you for overreacting or reading something into it when they claim that nothing is actually happening.

They will also use social media as a way to spy on you. Narcissists will often follow you on social media and pay attention to your goings-on online to see what you are doing and see anything that they could use against you. This helps them learn more about what you like, what you are interested in, and how you speak to your friends. Later, they will use this information in their love-bombing stage, where they attract your attention and get you to fall in love with them. Then, they will use this exact same information to abuse you by calling you names or ridiculing you for your various interests and the things you post or share.

Not only will a narcissist spy on you during the relationship and use the information against you, but they will also use it after the relationship ends as a way to stalk and harass you. If you have ever tried to leave the relationship in the past, you can likely recall them stalking everything you are doing and regularly messaging you, and trying to get in touch with you so that they could attempt to lure you back into the relationship. This is done in a way that is enough to feel like a clear violation but is typically not done so much so that it violates harassment laws enough to result in any type of persecution.

They will also use social media as a way to embellish their grandiose sense of self. They will post only images that they feel boost their popularity and social status as a way to feed their constant need for attention. Then, when they actually get likes, they will use this as a way to make others look lesser to them because they are not getting as much attention. Therefore, they can make it look like the other person is not cared about or likable. If you are in a relationship with these people, they will likely use you as a way to increase their popularity. For example, they may post provocative pictures of you or ones that make you look bad in some way but can be twisted to make them look good. This makes you look like the lesser person in the relationship and, as a result of their manipulation, makes them look like the good person even though they are posting pictures without your consent that show you off in a bad, uncomfortable, or inappropriate way. Not only does this feed their need to look good, but it can also further isolate you from others in your life because it may cause those you are close with to begin thinking less of you and believing that you are engaging in negative behavior, rather than the true fact which is that the person you were with exploited you and treated you abusively.

Lastly, social media provides an excellent platform for narcissists to bully and taunt other people. Online, narcissists take pleasure in provoking people to begin engaging in an argument but spin the entire thing to make it look like it is the other person's fault. They tend to be extremely cruel and violent, often threatening peoples' physical well-being or livelihood altogether.

Talks Behind People's Backs

Social media is not the only place where a narcissist will exploit their victims. Narcissists also like to talk behind people's backs when they are not around as a way to make them look better and create drama. One of the most frustrating things about this is that it can take an awfully long time before you realize this is happening. The narcissist is incredibly smart and tactical when it comes to these games. It becomes very painful and challenging to accept when you realize that these accusations and remarks about you are completely false. In virtually every scenario where you are not around, and the narcissist sees an opportunity to use you to increase their sense of self and harm your social image, they will. Typically, this talk will be degrading and will result in you being made out to sound like you are worthless, incapable, and despised, while the narcissist appears to always come out as the hero in the story. To them, it is a way of making themselves look great. For you, it can feel like they are making you sound like some form of an incompetent fool.

Energy Vampires

Because of their compulsive lying, the constant need for attention, addiction to drama, and their grandiose sense of self, narcissists are one of the highest forms of energy vampires. They require a lot of time and attention from other people, often resulting in them being willing to go to extreme lengths to get it. If you are in a relationship with them, they will naturally rely on you as their main energy source. When things become stagnant, the narcissist loves to create completely false accusations and situations to put you on the back foot and defend yourself. The narcissist loves creating drama and fights as a way to suck the energy out of you and make you work harder for their love and approval. As such, you may find yourself feeling constantly drained and exhausted by them. They will leach onto your energy until they can no longer do so because you are exhausted and have no energy left to give. Once they see you reach this weakened state, they will initiate the part of their abuse cycle where they begin to decimate your sense of self-esteem and self-confidence. This will drive you to a breaking point where you can no longer handle their abuse. Then, when you are just about ready to give up and find your freedom or peace, they come back with their love-bombing and try to refuel your energy tank. This results in a deep battle between you and them where you long to get away and feel free once again, but their energy vampire traits result in a vicious roller-coaster ride.

High Sex Drive

Energy is transferred in large amounts through sexual acts. For this reason, many narcissists have an incredibly high sex drive. They always want to have sex with you, exploit you during sex, and be made to feel like they are the "dominant" one during their sex with you. This is because they get a lot of energy out of this experience. It also is a great way for them to amplify the roller-coaster-like abuse cycle. If they have been super abusive to you lately and feel you slipping away from their web, they may try to love-bomb you with attention and sex. Because they are having sex with you, they will often make it seem like it will be a mutually enjoyable experience. That is until it begins. Once you start having sex with them, most of the time, they generally become selfish lovers and will only engage in the forms of sex that they want. If they do happen to give in to what you want, you can almost always guarantee that it will come back on you later as a situation where "I let you ____, so you owe me!" or "I did ____, which is proof of how much I love you!" type statements are used. This is a way to twist it to seem like they are generous and considerate of your feelings, but later they use this generosity to get their needs met and send yours down once again.

Inability to Feel Guilt or Remorse

As a result of their lack of empathy, narcissists are completely unable to feel guilty or remorseful for anything they have done. They are literally incapable, meaning that no matter what you do or say, they will never truly feel bad for their actions. However, this is not always apparent at first glance. In many instances, when it serves them, narcissists will *mimic* guilt or remorse as a way to make it appear as though they are genuinely sorry for what they have done or that they genuinely feel bad for creating chaos or destruction in your life in one way or another. This, however, is absolutely never a real sense of guilt or remorse. Instead, it is their way of getting you to believe that they did not have any ill intentions, thus allowing them to jump back on track to serve their own needs quickly. In some cases, they realize that arguing with you over their mistakes may take away too much from their end goal: to win. So, they will use their fake remorse as a way to avoid the hassle and get to where they want to be even faster. Plus, they can use this as "evidence" that they do feel bad when they hurt you, thus allowing them to make you sound crazy for believing that they always hurt you intentionally and without any concern. This keeps you roped in and believing their lies for as long as possible. Eventually, there will come a time when it is clearly evident that they are incapable of feeling remorseful or guilty for their actions. It is a painful truth to face, and it can be extremely difficult to comprehend how someone can be so cruel and numb. It is usually too late by this time, and you are deeply in the abuse cycle.

Inability to Apologize or Admit Wrong-Doing

One thing that you can guarantee about a narcissist is that they will never admit to being wrong. Narcissists do not, under any circumstances, apologize for their behavior or actions. They absolutely never will. If they do, you must never believe that this is a true admission of their mistake. Instead, they are using it as a bargaining chip to twist it around and make it sound like they made a mistake either because they were forced to (which transfers the blame away from them) or because it was supportive of the bigger picture (which in the end only feeds their needs and ego). The other time they will apologize is when you have done absolutely everything in your power to get them to apologize, and they have effectively sucked the life out of you, so they throw you a bone. But you can be sure there will be no truth or meaning to their apology. There is virtually never a sincere admission of a mistake from a narcissist. Why would they apologize to you when they don't even feel any sense of guilt or remorse for what they have done? Instead, they are more likely to lie and create another false sense of reality. Be aware of this.

Experts at Playing the Victim

Another trait narcissists carry as a result of being masters at manipulating is their ability to "turn the tables" and project onto others. Narcissists love to twist the switch around so that it seems like *you* were actually the one to do something that *they* did. For example, say you are in the middle of an argument, and a narcissist begins calling you names and bullying you.

If you were to later in the argument point this out and call them out on it, the narcissist would start projecting, saying that you were the one bullying them and anything they said was only a means of defending themselves against your bullying. This means that they can expertly become the victim of any situation and make you out to be the attacker. Because you are not the one playing the head games, but instead, you are the real victim, what can end up happening are two situations:

1. You feel the guilt and remorse that they are incapable of feeling. You will likely begin questioning your own actions and looking to verify what they have said. If they point out any specific evidence, you will immediately start feeling bad and trying to make up for what you have said or done, even though you likely never announced or did it with any malicious intent. As a result, they end up with the upper hand, and you are left apologizing to them and trying to make up for what you supposedly did when in reality, they are the ones behaving in an abusive manner. Or:

2. You are familiar with these games the narcissist plays and often, these false accusations and acts of victimization can lead to extreme cases of confusion and frustration. You can't even comprehend how the "tables are being turned" onto you now. Ultimately, your acts of confusion and frustration which can lead to more arguing and fighting are going to fuel the narcissist even more and significantly drain the energy out of you. Either way, the narcissist wins in this situation.

I hope this list of traits has been eye-opening for you and that you have been able to confidently identify a narcissist you may have in your life after reading this list of characteristics. Awareness is the first step. Once you know what you're dealing with, you can begin making the correct choices for your recovery.

The Signs You Are in a *Narcissist Relationship*

As you will see shortly, the major warning signs of a narcissistic relationship are all related to the traits of the narcissist and their behaviors. The narcissist is vain, superior, entitled, lacking in empathy, and prone to abuse. Narcissist is also extremely manipulative, so they will have a knack for getting you to see things their way. Indeed, because the narcissist's partner is often an empath, you may find that your emotions, viewpoints, and behaviors align with that of the narcissist to your detriment. The following is a review of warning signs that you are dealing with a narcissist.

- ✦ **You Recognize that You Are More Anxious or Depressed Than Is Typical for You**

The abuse of the narcissist will impact you in various ways in the relationship. One of the ways that you may be affected is that you start feeling more depressed or anxious. This occurs because the narcissist's belittling, demeaning, and manipulation causes you to lose self-esteem, making you depressed. You become anxious because the feelings resulting from the interaction with this person cause you to fear these interactions or even social interaction in general. Anxiety or depression of unknown cause is a telltale sign that you may have a narcissist in your life.

✦ Your Partner Has a Pattern of Diminishing Your Achievements and Advancing Their Own

It is essential to the narcissist that they constantly remind you (as well as remind themselves) that you are less than they are, and one of the ways they do this is by minimizing your achievements. It is very damaging to the self-esteem of a narcissist when they are met with the realization that they are not superior to others. Therefore, they prevent this from happening in close interpersonal relationships by tearing down the achievements of others or not recognizing them. However, their achievements will receive the attention the narcissist believes they deserve.

✦ You Recognize that Your Self-esteem Is Not as High as It Was in the Past

One of the most challenging aspects of dealing with a narcissist is that other people are not always aware of the sort of person into whose midst they have fallen. One way to tell that your significant other is a narcissist is that your self-esteem takes a plummet. Your self-esteem plummets not only because of the words the narcissist uses to belittle and demean you, but because of behaviors, the narcissist engages in—like ignoring your needs—that serve as a constant reminder that you are not their equal.

✦ You Are More Isolated from Others as a Result of Your Relationship

The narcissist will say and do things that drive a wedge between you and others. The narcissist may say that they are the only one who understands you, or that no one else cares about you as much as they do. How can the narcissist know this when they are not around for all of your actions? This is only a ploy used by the narcissist to control you. They want to be the only person of importance in your life, partly because they are codependent (as you may also be) and may require you to enable their mental illness, but also because they need someone to abuse.

✦ You Are the Target of Episodes of Rage from Your Partner

Unexpected episodes of rage are common in narcissistic relationships. Freud and other psychoanalysts believed that aggression was an important motivation for narcissists' behaviors. The narcissist is indeed motivated by a self-obsessed drive and an aggressive drive, but aggression can also stem from the narcissist not getting their way. The narcissist's rage is not unlike a child throwing a temper tantrum when the parent does not give them what they want, or their needs are not met immediately. Although narcissist is a calculating adult, they go into a rage for the same reason.

✦ Although You Spend More Time with Your Partner than with Others, You Feel Neglected and Ignored

Even though you are a participant in a codependent relationship, you will often feel ignored and neglected by your partner. This is because the emotional connection that you need and would normally have in a healthy relationship is missing in a narcissistic relationship. Instead of giving you the love and support that you expect, the narcissist uses their closeness to you to heal you and lift themselves up at your experience. The things that are missing from your relationship will leave you feeling ignored.

✦ You Are Always Wrong and Your Partner Is Always Right

The narcissist does not perceive you as being equal to them, and they will continuously remind you of this. One of the ways that they engage in this is to make sure you know that they are right and you are not. They may use the word "always" to describe your behaviors negatively. You are always messing things up. Or your intuition is always wrong.

On the other hand, the narcissist's wants and perceptions are always right. In reality, this is not true. This type of mind control is designed to place you deeper into the narcissist's hold.

✦ You Frequently Experience Comments or Behaviors that Demean and Belittle You

Demeaning and belittling are the favored weapons of the narcissist. Belittling is a way of reminding you of your subservient position. This is part of the codependency of narcissism as it subconsciously tells you that you need the narcissist when, in reality, they need you perhaps more than you need them. Demeaning also serves a role here. It weakens you, allowing the narcissist to continue to influence you in various ways.

✦ You Experience Periods of Hurtfulness as well as Acts of Charm or Love

The narcissist is not unlike the borderline person who can confuse those around them by frequently jumping back and forth between strong emotions like love and hate. The borderline person behaves this way because they have a mental illness stemming from dysfunctional development, but the narcissist does this because sometimes their mask of manipulation falls away, and you see them as they are. The signs of love that you receive from the narcissist are generally fake, designed to lure you into their control. The signs of dislike, anger and hurtfulness represent the narcissist's true self.

✦ You Feel Hollow at Times and You Do Not Know Why

Hollowness is a strange feeling that individuals with severe depression or other mental illnesses sometimes experience. It is a feeling of emptiness or a sort of out-of-body sensation that can result from severe mental disturbance, trauma, or both. This can happen in a narcissistic relationship because of the abuse trauma that the partner of the narcissist is subjected to. Often building up your self-esteem helps resolve this feeling of being hollow. Other times, distancing yourself from the narcissist is the only solution.

✦ You Notice that Your Partner Frequently Lies, Even When There Is No Obvious Benefit to Them of Their Lie

Narcissists are frequently pathological liars. Indeed, their entire persona is a lie. During the idealization phase, the narcissist convinced you that they were the answer to your prayers and that your life was better with them in it. This is the biggest lie of the narcissist. The narcissist will also lie in general conversations with you. They may do this to manipulate you, which happens commonly, or they may have no apparent reason for their lies. Lying has become a habit for them.

✦ **Nothing You Do Ever Seems to Meet the Demands of the Narcissist**

Whatever you do, it will never be enough for the narcissist. This is because narcissist has a self-image and worldview in which they are special. You are not special, so you will always be a disappointment to the narcissist. You will never meet their demands and they will remind you of this when they are not in the midst of trying to win you over.

✦ **You Experience Emotional Ups and Downs that Are Unexpected and Exhausting**

Being in a relationship with a narcissist can be akin to an emotional whirlwind. Aside from anxiety and depression, the partner of this person can fall victim to frequent bouts of crying, panic attacks, and other symptoms of hypersensitivity and excessive emotionality. Although the narcissist often chooses people who are naturally like this as partners, your innate propensity for emotionality will be exacerbated by the damaging behaviors of the narcissist.

✦ **Your Partner Always Manages to Reel You Back in When You Think You Have Had Enough**

The narcissist has few peers when it comes to manipulation. Just when you have reached your breaking point and have made the decision to call it quits, the narcissist will find a way to throw the lasso around your waist and bring you right back. They are able to do this for several reasons, of which one of the more important ones is the false self (the idealized self) that they constructed at the beginning of the relationship and which you wholeheartedly believe in despite all evidence that it is indeed false.

❖ Why We Attract Narcissists?

Many people wonder why they attract toxic people into their life. They wonder what signal is sent out that jerks and morally bankrupt people are answering. If you cannot wrap your head around the reason why you attract the wrong people, keep reading.

There are traits and characters in people that determine the kind of people that gravitates toward them. The vibe some people give acts like a sonar that can attract narcissists or other bad characters into their lives. This doesn't mean you are crazy or damaged; there is probably nothing wrong with you.

Just take note of the following:

Their Behavior Seems Normal

Some circumstances make a narcissist's behavior come off as "normal" or not as severe. If you grow up in a household surrounded by selfish and deeply flawed adults, such as narcissists, this behavior will feel normal and ideal to you.

Maybe you experienced physical or emotional abuse. You are used to everyone acting cold and in an atmosphere of hatred. You might grow up thinking it is okay for people to act that way. Any of this makes encountering a narcissist seems normal, and you are likely to accept their behavior.

You Regularly Crave Approval

When a narcissist has you in their sight, they will be on their best behavior. They will be the sweetest and most loving people you have ever met. Most times, they might even appear too good to be true. They shower you with attention and affection, and it seems like nothing you do is wrong.

However, once they feel you aren't going anywhere, they begin to criticize you, manipulate you, showing you their true colors. However, since we like to get the approval of people we care for, we bend over backward to please them and make them stay. This strengthens the bond and makes the narcissist see you as a source for restoring.

You Like Fixing People

A narcissist will give tales of pity in a bid to get on the good side of others. They will fabricate their stories to make it seem like every other person is responsible for their problems. If you are a caring, loving, and empathic person, you will take the bait and get yourself entangled to try and fix them.

They might come in the form of a drug addict, gambler, alcoholic, or someone just generally trying to find their footing. If you are fascinated by this person and fall in with them to try and change their life for the better, you will likely be sucked in until you break free.

You Don't Trust Yourself

If you do not have a good relationship with yourself, you can't expect to give in to your impulses and feelings without repercussions. You might end up attracting a narcissist. These kinds of people are considered prey to a narcissist because they will give you more reasons not to trust yourself. They will make you believe you are losing your grip on reality with manipulation and confusion.

In time, you will leave all of your trust in the hands of others and let them determine what is good and not good for you. You no longer have faith in your intuition, so you accept whatever the narcissists present to you. Narcissists thrive in such an environment, and you are sure to continue attracting these people unless you realize the problem and make a major change.

You Do Not Love or Value Yourself

A lack of self-love and value for yourself will make you reject advances from people who genuinely love and want to care for you. This mentality explains why you see no issue with poor treatment from others and you don't deserve this.

As a result, you feel powerless and helpless. You no longer find any value in taking care of yourself, so when someone comes along treating you the same way you already feel; you won't speak up. Narcissists can continue their abuse and mind games with little to no resistance from you.

Other people in your life are your mirrors. If you do not love yourself, you are less likely to find a responsible person who has enough of their own self-esteem to help. Remember that only narcissists, abusers, and toxic people find these traits alluring in other people.

You Have Low Self-Worth

If one of the significant tactics employed by a narcissist is manipulation, then it is more likely that people with low self-worth are their bread and butter. These virtues are like a magnet because they provide a perfect environment for the narcissist. A narcissist will prey on your insecurities and keep you focused on them to make you believe you deserve the abuse.

Since you are not secure and grounded in yourself, you will not question them. Also, you subconsciously believe the horrible things you hear from your abuser and even accept them.

You Ignore the Red Flags

We might not want to be skeptical of every person we meet. We can't act crazy and believe people are out to get us. We might want to believe in the basic goodness of man and believe everyone has good intentions. We also don't want to face the harsh reality of an otherwise ideal partnership, so we ignore red flags.

This might come in the form of downplaying the bad behavior of that toxic person. You may rationalize and try to make excuses for their behavior. A narcissist will see you as gullible and play on your intelligence. Since you won't challenge their behavior, it gives them free rein to do what they want.

We explained why you might attract a narcissist. You are neither crazy nor stupid. Narcissists exist in the world, and there is nothing you or this book can do about it other than educate. You can protect yourself from being a victim of their careless whims. You can take steps to check the habits that attract them and take appropriate steps to change them. It is time you stop narcissists from controlling your life.

A Narcissist Weakness Points

Narcissists are far from invincible. Their most terrifying traits are also their weakest spots. You can leverage those traits that make them detrimental and start to point them out to you first, then to them. The first step is to get your independence straight first - any kind of independence. Afterward, when you decide that you're mentally ready, elevate your inner peace, put a confident smile on your face, and be armed with tranquil logic, get ready for the battle that you're going to win.

My advice is to be ready to leave, especially if the narcissist is beyond being worth the extra effort. To understand this, watch out for threats from your partner. It might be a threat to leave you, to blackmail you, or another out-out threat, which is very common when dealing with a narcissist. Watch out for statements like:

- "If you do not do this by ____, consider this relationship over."
- "Everyone will know what kind of person you are."
- "I am better off without you; go ahead and leave."

✦ Excessive Need for Attention and Validation

If your partner has a high need for validation, you are probably dealing with a narcissist. They will try every means to get your attention. To a narcissist, external validation is important for them to feel good and wanted. Stop his narcissistic flow: he doesn't need to do whatever it is that it's hurting you to have your respect.

If you don't stop the bleeding, validation will never be enough. Even though they so crave validation and approval from you, there is no end. No matter how much you let them know you care for them and approve of them, it won't soothe them, as it's very difficult for them to appreciate and see anyone truly loving them. This can be traced to the root of narcissism because despite being self-absorbed, they are insecure deep down—hence the desire for more and more approval.

✦ A Huge Need for Control

A narcissist is never happy with life. This makes him try all in his capacity to mold things to his liking. As a result of this, they have a compulsion for control. Their sense of entitlement also makes it logical for them to want to be in control.

A narcissist has an idealized way in which people should act. When people fail to behave as expected, it upsets them. Since you've already deviated, they are clueless about what to expect next, which throws them off balance. Explain that life sometimes is beautiful exactly because it cannot be controlled.

Narcissists want you to act and do as they please so they can reach their idealized conclusion. To them, you are just a pawn to achieve their selfish desire—a robot that should be controlled and told what to do! Let them know you really enjoy deciding your next step.

✦ Inability to Accept Responsibility

While narcissists strive to be in control, they also tend to dodge responsibility for the outcome. This only change if the result goes as expected; otherwise, they feel inadequate and place all the blame on you. Accepting fault is never in their nature, as they just have to deflect.

Sometimes the blame could be generalized—the government, the law enforcement agent, the caregivers, etc. Other times, a particular person could be the object of his blame, like his parents, colleague, boss, etc. Most times, however, the blame falls on the person most emotionally close to the narcissist. Show them that being accountable for what one did wrong is just a step to being a better human, it means growing.

They cannot do without blaming, as it helps keep up with their idealized sense of perfection. The only problem is 1) Perfection is unattainable; perfection is not perfect.

✦ Perfectionism

In the narcissist's little world though, they are perfect. As a result, they expect you and everyone else to be perfect. Narcissists have this invisible script well planned out in their heads, dictating how things should go.

Events, life, and people around them must follow this carefully crafted script just like they wrote it.

This, without a doubt, is an impossible demand, which eventually makes the narcissist miserable and dissatisfied. It is important to make them notice their helplessness and to really think about a moment they were happy if there were one. I bet that world domination was not in the equation.

✦ Emotional Reasoning

You might be frustrated about the behavior of your partner. You tried everything in your effort to explain to him and make him see how much pain and suffering he is causing you. You expect he will adjust if he understands how much he's hurting you. But since a narcissist is only caught up in his world, your explanations make little to no sense to him. Even if he admits he understands, he really does not.

Thus, narcissists' actions and decisions are usually based on how they feel. The only reason they need to get the latest sports car is how driving it makes them feel. They are not bothered by the fact that it is a burden on the family and budget. At the slightest provocation and discomfort, a narcissist could quit his job with the hope of moving to another one or starting a business. To a narcissist, their problem can only be solved by something or someone else, not themselves. Think about it: this gives you great powers upon him. In their mind, you are responsible for their happiness. If they cannot embrace accountability, you will have to use this to your advantage. You can become the boss of this relationship anytime.

✦ Fear And Anxiety

The life of a narcissist revolves around fear, yet for most of them, this fear is deeply buried. They fear being wrong, being seen as incapable, not being accepted, etc. They fear being fired, being tested, being considered inadequate. It is because of this fear that a narcissist hardly trusts anyone.

The deeper your relationship gets, the more he becomes suspicious of you. Narcissists have a phobia of true intimacy as it makes them vulnerable, which could expose their weak points. All your assurance and reassurance make no difference, as their imperfection is a personal turnoff.

Make use of the Pygmalion effect: the them they're good, that you expect them to be great at what they're doing, that you expect them to love you, and they will surely do it. Do as an expert fisherman would; let the line out a little bit, make them think they won, it will discombobulate their certainties.

✦ An Inability to be Vulnerable

Since a narcissist cannot truly process feelings and always needs to protect their image, it is difficult for them to truly connect with others. Since they are full of themselves and their ways, they cannot consider things from another person's perspective. Emotionally, they are lonely, which makes them needy.

When a relationship does not give them what they want, they pull the plug and jump to the next one as soon as possible. Wired deep in their DNA is the need to always make everything as they want it, have someone feel their pain, and sympathize with them. On the contrary, however, they are not capable of responding to someone else's needs.

My suggestion is if a fellow human being is not capable of feeling the value of being vulnerable after a number of attempts have been made, you have the duty to protect yourself and decide to find more worthy companions for your journey.

Relationships with a Narcissist

Relationships of all kinds with narcissists follow three stages: **Love bombing**, **devaluing**, and **discarding**. This predictable cycle is followed regardless of what type of relationship is forged with the narcissist; narcissists will repeat this with romantic partners, children, friends, and anyone else in their lives who accept it. Those who do not accept it are either demeaned and attacked or completely disregarded and dismissed. While the three stages are followed, narcissists' behavior changes somewhat depending on the kind of relationship and what is socially acceptable within those relationship's norms.

❖ Different Types Of Abusive Behavior

Narcissists have endless ways they abuse others. They use abuse to get people in line and ensure that they get their way. Though the toxic narcissist, in particular, prefers to abuse people for sport, most times, narcissistic abuse is opportunistic. The narcissist is using it as a tool or a weapon against his victim. He does not care what the result is, but he is not necessarily doing it to be mean-spirited intentionally or just to hurt someone; the harm is collateral damage in manipulating the other person into doing what he wants. His end goal is typically getting whatever he desires, not hurting people. Most narcissists are far too interested in their own feelings to worry about hurting other people just to hurt them, and narcissists are typically much more preoccupied with themselves anyway. Nevertheless, all of these manipulation techniques have the potential to inflict serious physical or emotional harm if used against other people. This list is by no means comprehensive, but these are some of the most commonly used abuse tactics.

Physical

Narcissists, when they are unable to get their way through manipulation, do not shy away from physical abuse. Sometimes, the narcissist simply can no longer control his anger, particularly the toxic or closet narcissists, and he lashes out physically in an attempt to physically force you into submission. He may take away your phone to prevent you from calling for help or breaking things to scare you, or he may even physically harm you.

The narcissist does not feel bad about hurting other people; even if you are in a relationship with him, he sees nothing wrong with his actions. The narcissist only cares about getting his results; if hitting you is the only thing that will work at the moment, then the narcissist will do it.

Hitting you, throwing stuff at you, destroying your things, pulling your hair, sexually exploiting you, etc., all come under this category.

Sexual

This type of covert aggression involves flattering you just to get what the narcissist wants. He may tell you that you look beautiful five minutes before demanding you do something tedious for him. The flattering or seduction is not genuine and is strictly used to warm you up, so you are more willing to do whatever the narcissist wants.

While this may not seem outward or even inwardly aggressive, the aggressive nature of this lies in the fact that the narcissist is toying with your emotions, using them to get whatever it is that he wants from you. He is essentially using you, your emotions, and your ego as a tool to get what he wants. He has treated you as little more than a means to an end, which is dehumanizing and cruel.

Verbal/Emotional

Verbal abuse intends to break down the target into submission. It is frequently used to make the other person feel insecure enough that they give in simply because they do not feel as though they are worthy of anything else. Verbal abuse has many different forms that it can take, and all of them are particularly harmful and serves to make the victim wonder if they are to blame or if they are overreacting in general.

Verbal abuse almost always takes place in private since no one else is around to hear or witness it, allowing the narcissist to deny its existence if necessary. This also creates an isolation effect on the victim, as the victim feels as though he or she cannot reach out to others because there is no proof of what was said. Verbal abuse may not often happen at first, but it eventually escalates to the point that it is a typical method of communication, particularly when in private.

The victims of verbal abuse frequently rationalize the abuse as being an acceptable form of communication, but it is still difficult for the victims to deal with at the moment. They may not recognize that it is essentially another form of exerting control over the situation and over the victim.

There are several different types of verbal abuse, some of which are easier than others to identify. Here are several abuse patterns as well as an example of what they may look like at the moment:

- **Name-calling:** "Wow, you're such an idiot! You never learn, do you?"
- **Manipulation:** "If you loved me, you would do this for me, even if you don't want to."
- **Demeaning comments:** "Wow, you're such a typical girl—you can't even remember to get your oil changed in your car. No wonder it broke down again."
- **Condescending:** "Hah, no wonder you always complain about struggling with your schoolwork—you can't even figure out how to double a recipe!"
- **Unconstructive, cruel criticism:** "Can't you do anything right? You're always able to bring down the mood with one stupid mistake, aren't you?"
- **Threats:** "You won't like what happens if you do that." Or "I will kill myself if you ever try to leave."
- **Blame:** "It's your fault we never have any money for anything fun." Or "Look at what you made me do! I would never have done it if you had just listened."
- **Silent treatment:** Your partner intentionally avoids talking to you to make you miserable.

Not all verbal abuse can be tagged as narcissistic. You must look at the context, frequency, and spite (hatred/vengeance) in the behavior since people often criticize, interrupt, blame, be sarcastic, oppose, block or blame you depending on what the situation may be. You must assess the frequency of this behavior. Bullying, name-calling, shaming, belittling, demanding, blaming, threatening, criticizing, getting violent, accusing, undermining, and orders are all verbal abuse.

Psychological Gaslighting

Emotional blackmail is common in most relationships these days. People have learned the art of using sensitive statements or emotions to make their partner think that their partner is wrong. Emotional blackmail is another form of manipulation and may include punishment, anger, threats, intimidation, or warning.

Gaslighting involves the act of convincing someone else that their understanding of reality is skewed or inaccurate in some way. The narcissist is a master at gaslighting, and it is one of his most frequently wielded manipulative weapons. The narcissist will seek to make you doubt yourself, slowly at first, until you are so certain that you cannot be trusted that the narcissist can take control of everything. Because you may doubt yourself so much that you no longer trust yourself to make important decisions, you will rely more on your partner. This also makes you far more likely to stay in the relationship, as you will not trust that what you think happened actually did. You will listen when the narcissist downplays it or tells you that it was not what you think it was.

Typically, this starts out slowly, with the narcissist making your belief seem like a harmless mistake. For example, you may tell him that your car keys are on the key holder, and he will correct you a few minutes later, saying they were actually on the counter, even if they were, in fact, on the key holder. It escalates slowly until the victim eventually believes anything the narcissist says.

Each incident of gaslighting will follow a specific pattern: Something happens. The narcissist either has a distorted view of what has happened, such as him being the victim in an argument that he started, or he creates a distorted view that will fit his narrative, even if he knows it is false. The narcissist then convinces the victim of his distorted truth. The victim then believes the narcissist.

Narcissists may try one of the following methods to gaslight you into submission:

- **Withholding:** The narcissist refuses to hear your side of things or pretends that your side of the story does not make sense.

- **Countering**: The narcissist directly counters or questions the victim's perception of what has happened, questioning if it is accurate.

- **Diverting**: The narcissist changes the subject and accuses the victim of misremembering.

- **Trivializing**: The narcissist makes the victim feel as though what the victim is saying or feeling is unimportant or delegitimizes them.

- **Denying**: The narcissist feigns having forgotten what has happened or denies anything that the victim says, saying it is falsified or made up on purpose.

Financial/Economic

The financial abuser who does not endorse a plan that best suits everyone in the family would leave those who are financially vulnerable. On the other hand, a person who loves his family is a protector, one who will make every effort to meet the needs of all family members—even before himself. This is what love for spouses and parents looks like.

A narcissist will always try to convince you he is the victim: even if it doesn't look like it in the present, he has a master plan, and what he's doing, he's doing it for you. You just don't see it yet. Politely ask to explain every little detail of the plan, so that even you can understand it. As the word etymology says, a couple works with two individuals coming together. If he wants to work alone, you're not, obviously, a couple. Easy.

Cultural/Identity

The narcissist, a master of manipulation, frequently casts out bait to get his way. He will lull you into complacency, making you feel as though your relationship is stable and comfortable, only to bait you into inciting an argument. Oftentimes, the bait involves something you are sensitive about. The narcissist may know that you are sensitive about being cheated on in the past, for example, so the next time you are out, he may look at another person, intentionally appearing obviously interested in the other person. He may even go and flirt with the other person in an attempt to make you feel jealous.

When you inevitably call him out, he will deny having ever done anything like what you are insisting on. He will say that he has no interest in the other person and turn it into an argument about your own insecurities. He has essentially tricked you into an argument, and when anyone asks, he will tell the world that you constantly accuse him of cheating when he has no interest in being anything other than a perfect partner.

This has allowed the narcissist to create a victim narrative after baiting you into acting irrationally, and he will use that cast bait any time he can. He wants to make you feel as though you are the irrational, abusive one.

❖ What Is Emotional Abuse?

Determining whether someone has gone through abuse might require some careful observation and investigation because abuse, in whatever form, will always show. Therefore, people often end up thinking that physical abuse is the worst form because the scars usually appear on the surface. However, people who have gone through emotional abuse would beg to differ with the notion that their invisible cuts do not go so deep since theirs could very well be the worst form. The heart and the mind are fragile, and breaking them will always lead to serious negative consequences. Here is an in-depth look into emotional abuse and its relationship with narcissism.

Definition

Emotional abuse, also called psychological abuse, mental abuse, or chronic verbal aggression, is any act or treatment that diminishes a person's dignity and worthiness. Emotional abuse is very broad and can take very many forms, including name-calling, statements, threats, intimidation, and even actions such as dismissiveness, spying, and silent treatment. More often than not, one person having full control over another person characterizes it.

A person can be abusive in very many ways. In most cases, though, abuse is either physical abuse or emotional abuse. Marks and physical pain are characteristics of physical abuse. It is very easy to comprehend and realize. Emotional abuse, on the other hand, can be very hard to spot, as it leaves emotional scars that are difficult to see.

Individuals in emotionally abusive environments may not even know that they are in abusive situations. However, if there is a repetitive pattern of mistreatment, then chances are that the emotional abuse is clear, if not to the victim herself but the people around her. The occasional arguments, outbursts, teasing, and dramatic behavior may or may not constitute emotional abuse.

What makes a person find out that he or she is in an emotionally abusive situation is his or her feelings toward the other person's actions. If a relationship makes you feel small, scared, anxious, voiceless, insecure, and isolated, then there is a likelihood that you are in an emotionally abusive relationship.

Where It Happens

Emotional abuse can occur anywhere and in our various interactions with other people. It can occur in the following ways:

- Intimate relationships—Men and women can be emotionally abusive to each other while dating or in their marriages. Emotional abuse in relationships may or may not lead to or include physical abuse.

- Friendships—There are very many cases where friends are emotionally abusive towards one another, especially where one believes to be superior to another.

- Family setup—A parent, caregiver, or older sibling can abuse the younger members of the family. Studies reveal that a caregiver or parent that went through some form of abuse as a child is likely to be abusive to his or her child when they grow up. Children or relatives can also be emotionally abusive to the elderly in the family.

- Workplaces—A coworker or boss can be emotionally abusive, although emotional abuse in the office is more common among young people, women, and uneducated people.

- School—Children tend to bully one another in school, among the different forms of emotional abuse. A teacher can also be verbally abusive towards students and vice versa.

Effects of Emotional Abuse

Emotional abuse may never lead to physical abuse, but the consequences of the act can be just as bad as inflicting physical pain on a person. Sometimes emotional abuse is far worse than physical abuse and may take longer to recover from than physical pain. Prolonged emotional abuse can lead to the following:

- Low self-esteem—this leads to people lacking confidence and feeling bad about themselves.

- Personality changes—people going through such abuse can change from being very jovial and talkative to becoming gloomy and reserved.

- Depression—as a result of depression, people think, feel, and act sad, appearing to have lost interest in the things they used to love.

- Anxiety—these people end up developing intense and persistent worry about most things in their lives, especially where the abuser is involved.

- Health issues such as ulcers, palpitations, and eating disorders—these health issues can be the result of stress, depression, and giving up on life.

- Suicidal thoughts—getting to this point is a sure sign that someone needs help because they think the only way out of their situation is through death.

- Psychological trauma—emotional abuse can cause stress that can be so overwhelming that an individual cannot cope with it, therefore leading to psychological trauma.

WHAT TO DO

We need to treat each other with respect, whether we're a child or a grown-up. If you are in an abusive relationship or situation, you should realize that it is not your fault that you are in the circumstances that you find yourself in; it is the abuser's fault. You also do not deserve other people treating you in a demeaning way. After having done your considerations, if you suspect or know that you are in an emotionally abusive relationship, you can take the following steps to discontinue any further emotional abuse.

Speak to someone else. If you think you may be in an emotionally abusive relationship, you can reach out to a friend, partner, family member, or counselor who can give his or her own perspective on the relationship.

Be honest with yourself, acknowledge and accept the fact that you are in an emotionally abusive environment and that something needs to change. Never blame yourself or think that you are the problem, which is why your abuser picks on you.

Confront your abuser and ask them to stop the mistreatment. Be very firm with them and establish boundaries. Clearly, spell out the consequences of crossing a certain line. If the person continues abusing you emotionally, take action and do what you must do.

Do not try to fix an abusive person or wait for them to change. Most abusive people have deep-rooted issues that require professional help to understand and fix. You are only responsible for your actions and not those of other people.

Never feel obligated to stay in an emotionally abusive relationship or situation. Work on an exit strategy and leave. Staying in a toxic relationship will eventually take a toll on you.

Seek help. Talking to a professional or trusted friend or close family member about what you have gone through can help you to recover faster.

Seven Signs of Emotional Abuse

People who are the closest to us they're the ones most likely to inflict emotional abuse. It can be a friend, partner, parent, caregiver, coworker, or business partner. Although the signs of emotional abuse are obvious, some people may be too deep into a relationship to realize that they are being emotionally abused. Others may be in denial of the fact that they are in an emotionally abusive situation, while some others may choose to ignore it. Whatever your situation is, you do not have to put up with emotional abuse. Here are patterns of abusive people that you can identify and make a decision to get away from.

1) They insult and humiliate you in any of the following ways:

- Emotionally abusive people tend to be verbally abusive. They call their victims all sorts of names. Name-calling is blatantly one of the signs of emotional abuse.
- They also call you degrading pet names. This is another way of name-calling.
- They use curse words when addressing you. Speaking to a person while you curse and swear is insulting. It also shows a lack of respect.
- Emotional abusive people can use sarcasm frequently whenever they talk to you.
- They tell bad jokes about you. Some people say that some things said as a joke may actually be true. Whether this is true or not, bad jokes tend to be humiliating.
- They patronize you. A good example of a person being patronizing is when they talk slowly at you because they think that you cannot comprehend what is being said.
- They constantly criticize your physical appearance. Some emotional abusers constantly comment on your body, your wardrobe choice, and your hairstyle.
- They cheat and shamelessly lie to you and expect to get away with it.
- They refuse to recognize your intellect.
- They like to humiliate you in public.

2) They are unpredictable in the sense that:

- They start arguments about anything and everything, at any place and at any time. They bring up an argument over a very small matter.

- They have mood swings. A person who is loving one minute and full of anger and rage the minute later is a person to stay away from.

- They have emotional outbursts.

- They are destructive. When angry, they throw items on the floor or wall. This is dangerous because they may end up throwing an object at you.

- They are two-faced; they are very polite and jovial in public but change the minute they get into the car to go home.

3) They accuse and blame you for just about anything:

- An abusive person seems to be always lecturing you.

- They accuse you of certain behaviors that you do not engage in.

- They are good at turning the tables on you. They make it appear as if you are the bad person or the one who makes a big deal of nothing. They also pretend not to see the sense in what you are saying.

- They blame you for causing them to be upset.

- They portray themselves as the victims.

- They can never be at fault.

4) They are intimidating:

- An abusive person yells when talking to you to let you know that they are the ones in control.

- They treat you like a child.

- They give orders rather than make a request.

- They demand respect rather than earn it.

- They always threaten to do something to you or themselves.

- An abusive person treats you as inferior.

- They dismiss your needs and emotions.
- They label you as needy if you insist on getting attention.
- They push your buttons so that they can upset you, start a confrontation, and shut you down.
- They gaslight you, making you question your own sanity.

5) Take control of every aspect of your life:

- An abusive person will want to monitor your call, texts, emails, and whereabouts. Chances are that they have access to all your passwords.
- They make all the decisions without consulting or discussing them with you.
- They control the finances and demand that your account for every cent you spend.
- They withhold affection and use it to blackmail you.
- They constantly remind you of their importance in your life and what you stand to lose if they decide to leave.

6) Ignore your presence, feelings, emotions, and needs:

- They tend to dismiss you when you bring up an issue or want to talk to them.
- Abusive people interrupt you when you speak, or they walk away.
- They do not communicate. They do not answer calls or texts, yet they expect you to be available when they reach out.
- They are not aware of your feelings. They do not share in your joy and pain.

7) Isolate you from your friends, family, and coworkers:

- They insist that you should spend all your time with them.
- They control who you talk to, see and how long you do it.

- They want to know where you are all the time.
- They like to turn others against you.
- They think little of your friends and family.
- They make it extremely difficult for you to see people or keep in touch. They can delete a contact.
- They accuse you of cheating to get you to stay indoors.

Never encourage or put up with emotional abuse by telling yourself that your situation is not as bad as it seems. Emotional abuse will affect you in the long run. In extreme cases, it can also escalate to physical abuse or lead to death.

The Dark Empath

The dark empath is to be considered, in all respects, the perfect predator. A dark empath personality mixes the traits of the "dark triad" with the ability to understand others' emotions. So not only a narcissist but add Machiavellianism and psychopathy to the mix. They are not just energy vampires; they won't just drain your energy; they will brood and plot while caring about your feelings. Consider a dark empath as the beautiful fallen angel, he will get under your skin if you just let him. When a psychopath is bestowed with the ability to understand others' emotions, we face an emotional manipulation expert.

Given their compound abilities, they are so good at being manipulative that it can take months before they make the first move! It combines all the characteristics of the manipulator, with whom we have all had to deal at least once in our lives and have learned about, with the characteristics of an empath with his understanding of human feelings. The most striking difference between a narcissist, sociopath, or psychopath and the dark empath is so simple that it could chill the blood in your veins.

While the former cannot feel and empathize with the "victim," the latter, the so-called dark empath, clearly has the spectrum of sensations and feelings that the person in front of him is feeling but does not care about. They will have the patience, the ability, and the capacity to enter your life on tiptoe and to be able to change your perception of the world without you noticing.

They are dangerous, but only if they want to be so. They are the demonstration that empathy is not a good absolute, but just a means to an end.

Let's take a look at the traits that you can find in a dark empath.

They are on the extrovert side. Usually, a dark empath shows himself as very social, even though that may not be his true nature. Their empathic part gives them knowledge of what it takes to have high social skills. They tend not to shy away from expressing their thoughts or views, especially those with opposite opinions.

It has been noted that most of them do not possess normal empathy; rather, they use what is called "cognitive empathy." They don't necessarily feel what others are feeling, but they always know what they are feeling. When they connect with people, they will usually end up exploiting them.

They enjoy power. They have an inclination to always want to be the leader in the environment they find themselves in. Why? Because they enjoy it, not because they want to lead. They want people to know they're the boss but tend to avoid the responsibilities and duties that the role requires. On the brighter side, this can lead them to bring the best out of those around because interpreting the role of the boss and forming good subordinates solidifies their leading position.

They uphold their pride above anything else. Dark empaths tend to have a superiority complex, so much that it represents one of their weakest points. This is their narcissist side coming to the surface, which often results in indirect aggression.

They are talented. Not all is bad in these individuals. In fact, they are found to have remarkable talents in certain aspects of life. For example, they are very persistent, they are able to make quick decisions, which makes them look like genuine leaders. Of course, that doesn't mean that they always take the best decisions. They are also talented in making people think they are on the same side. They can be perfect populist politicians or negotiators, yet often there's no substance behind their words.

They're good at guild-tripping people. As they're very good at manipulating people's emotions, they can also use this ability to guilt-tripping people. They use empathy as an instrument for placing others on the stand, appointing themselves in the role of the good mentor, ready to give advice.

They use poisonous humor. One of the classic traits of a dark empath. Their superiority complex must be fueled by malicious humor toward others. The obscure empath makes fun or laughs at those he considers beneath him, and it's a humor aimed to belittle while feigning sympathy, destructive in nature. He will use hurtful jokes to put someone down while seeking for compliance from everybody else.

Not all dark empaths are inclined toward evil-doing, though. One can simply have empathic abilities cohabit with the dark triad, and still choose to use the mix for good.

Narcopath

A narcopath is a narcissist-sociopath mix and is considered the worst type. Someone with a hyper-inflated ego, full of how important they are, as well as a constant need for praise and admiration, which already sounds exhausting! Relationships with them can be addictive but draining as the person with a narcopath will never end up winning in anything.

Here is an excellent checklist for identifying whether you are involved with a narcopath:

1. Things move fast, really fast! Instead of getting to know you, a narcopath will immediately make you feel like you've found your soul mate.

2. The compliments: At first, they might feel nice, but after a while, you might realize that they're generic and maybe a bit staged.

3. Flattery comes in the form of comparisons. It is especially bad if it links to an ex. Even if you come out on top, that won't last.

4. You have strong chemistry. The passion is off the charts, but not much else is good.

5. Hollow eyes that lead to nothing. It's all an act.

6. Here's a big one: conversations always swivel back to themselves.

7. A checkered relationship history is a sign of things to come.

8. The silent treatment is standard.

This is another severe form of narcissism that can lead to abuse and violence if left untreated. It isn't always easy to confront someone who behaves in such a way, but doing so can lead to a happier future for the perpetrator and everyone in their life. Some therapy, especially cognitive behavioral therapy, can help with this.

The red flags of manipulation by a narcopath include:

- Your words are being used against you.
- They offer you help, but their support leaves you confused and unhappy.
- They say shocking things, then claim that you misunderstood them.
- A lot of what they do is designed to make you feel guilty and shame.
- You question your sanity.
- Love and affection are withdrawn once you don't obey them.
- You fear losing that person, no matter what they do (°this may also lead to a form of Stockholm syndrome)
- You always feel like you fall short of expectations.
- You have been on eggshells with that person.
- You feel isolated by them.

If you feel any of these things happening in your life, you need to start thinking about taking some serious action.

If times get tough, here are some suggestions to implement aspects of your abuser's personality that can help you fighting who makes you suffer the most and survive the period you have to deal with him.:

- Establish your own identity; don't worry about what others expect of you.
- Feel proud when you reach your goals.
- Listen to and read affirmations.
- Consider what you like about yourself.
- Care for yourself.

- Be kind to yourself, but also keep being good to others.

- Allow yourself to have imperfections.

- When you feel bad, please do something to change it. You are who controls your mental state, always.

- Share in the success of others. Use them as examples, and be part of their happiness.

Defeat Your Fear

HOW TO HANDLE A NARCISSIST

From the previous chapters, we have been analyzing the characteristics of a narcissist and the impact this person has on any relationship through the lenses of the empathic individual. So, it is safe to say that at this point, you know precisely what you are dealing with and the importance of you escaping the situation for good.

The narcissist has an internalized motto, "me first," and he isn't entirely concerned about you or your emotions which further explains why you must be willing to make the required changes that will help you deal with the situation and get out of it for good.

You may not know it, but you are being emotionally drained every second and minute you spend with a narcissist. The more dedicated you are to such a relationship, the more you give away your emotional freedom.

So, it is time to say, "**Enough!**".

The objective of this chapter is to present the top eight steps that will help you handle a narcissist. We will explore some of the most effective approaches aimed at helping you regain control over your life. You must take the lessons learned in this chapter seriously because it is the crucial part that will make your life better.

See Them for Who They Are

If you are an empathic person, it would be easier for you to ignore some of the warning signs exhibited through the characteristic display of a narcissist. In some cases, you may even find yourself making excuses for the individual, not because you are not aware of their wrong behavior, but because you are empathic, and it is in your nature to seek the good in others.

But you must understand that we are dealing with a particular issue here, and as such, you are required to handle the situation objectively and not emotionally. This means that you must see this narcissist for who he is and accept the reality.

Narcissists know when to turn on their charm, especially when they realize that you are upset with them, and before you know it, you are drawn to them again.

But before you go right back to them, think about how they treated other people and the other negative emotional and physical manifestations they displayed. Now with all that they have done, it is glaringly obvious that they lack emotional awareness, and you need to make your peace with that.

Do not think about the idealized version of the person you would rather have; instead, look at how he is now and accept that this person has some deep-rooted issues that must be handled, otherwise, they will snowball into a catastrophic experience.

This is not the time to be delusional about a person's capabilities, nor is it a time to exercise patience because we are talking about who a person is and what he is capable of doing.

Until you accept them for who they are, you will never be able to take on the other steps that help you find the solution. Yes, you've got seven other steps below, but I am telling you now that without this first step, you cannot succeed with the others.

Accepting the narcissist for who he is will help protect you emotionally from the hurt and abuse that may be thrown at you. When you don't accept the reality of this person's character, you will be surprised, stunned, and significantly hurt every time he says or does something to you.

But when you accept the person's state, nothing done to you will be a surprise; you will have the upper hand in the relationship because you are mentally, emotionally, and physically prepared for whatever may happen.

This step which entails seeing a person for who he is, can be very frustrating for the narcissist. Narcissist's love being in control, so when they sense that you are no longer riled up by their antics, they will have a first clue that they'd better learn to behave appropriately around you.

No one can change a person unless the person in question decides to make changes; what you can do is influence them to make changes, and for you to achieve that, you must come to terms with the reality of the person's situation.

Who are you building a relationship with? Has the person shown narcissistic tendencies toward you? Have you been making excuses for this individual? Then it is time to accept this person for who he is before we can discuss the next step that we should take toward handling the issue.

When a person tries to get over an addiction, the first thing they make the person do is admit to being an addict and then help roll in. You cannot reach out to someone else if they haven't come to terms with who they are, so before we move on to the next step, quietly accept that this person is a narcissist and get ready to free yourself emotionally from their controlling grasp.

✓ *DO NOT MAKE YOUR SELF-WORTH DEPENDENT ON THEM*

After accepting who they are, you need to ensure that you no longer make your self-worth dependent on them. Because narcissists are quite demanding, it is effortless for empathic individuals to give in to their demands, sometimes even subconsciously, because they are emotionally invested in the narcissist.

So now that you know who this person is and you have accepted the facts, it is time to change your emotional connection and the impact the individual may have on your self-worth. Put a stop to your psychological dependence on them by not trying to please them all the time.

A narcissist will never stop taking from you; he only knows how to take and not give, so if you think that this pattern will end, you are very wrong, which is why, as you read, you must commit to not placing the power of your self-worth in that person's hand.

Also, protect your sensitivity by refraining from sharing your feelings with a person who doesn't care or cherish them. A person's self-worth gets automatically damaged when he continually seeks attention and emotional care from someone else who doesn't provide that.

So, if you are keen on building a stronger emotional bond with yourself and with those who truly care about you, you will need to cut off the influence this person has over you and how you feel about yourself.

Your self-worth is just that—yours—and this narcissist needs to understand that. Another reason why you might have been dependent on this individual enough for it to affect your self-worth is that you are entirely focused on them.

Narcissists work hard to keep themselves in the spotlight at the expense of other people, so without even realizing it, you will discover that throughout the relationship, you have pushed your needs aside to keep them satisfied. This process leaves a massive dent in your self-worth, and to correct the issue, you must redirect your attention to yourself and others who matter and care about you.

Don't allow a narcissist to infiltrate your sense of self or define your emotional balance. Tell yourself, "I matter too," and regularly remind yourself of your strengths, goals, and desires. No matter what happens, you must be the center of attraction in your own life.

If you observe that this narcissist is always around you, then create "me time" for yourself and make it clear that you are now taking care of yourself first. It is not your job to try and fix anyone else or have misplaced emotional priorities because someone else refused to own up to their issues.

Your responsibility is first to yourself before others, and it has to be to people who love, care and value you while you are working on self-worth. Remember to speak up!

✓ *SPEAK UP!*

Most of the time, narcissists are so self-absorbed that they won't notice the little non-verbal signs and hints you share with them indicating your frustration in the relationship. If you continually rely on those signs, you will never handle the situation because guess what, the narcissist doesn't care!

If the narcissist doesn't pay attention to those hints you share, you will have to be proactive by speaking up and being expressive. Now, because you are dealing with an individual who can easily dismiss what you say, you need to think of a way to get his attention.

Don't tell the narcissist, "We need to talk," before sharing what's on your mind. When you give them a notice for a discussion before the discussion happens, they come prepared, ready to steal the show, and you will be left defenseless.

So, the best way to speak up to a narcissist is to SPEAK UP!

Just walk up to him and say what needs to be said. When you do this, you will catch the person unaware and fully be in control of the situation. It might take the narcissist a longer time to bounce back and try to manipulate you, but before then, you have already said your piece. Now it is also important to note that with this step, you are not going to have a conversation with this person; this isn't the time for discussions that will allow the narcissist to create a scene with that big-sized ego.

Instead, you are going to TALK to him, you are going to get some things off your chest and lay out the things that have been bothering you while insisting on a change in behavior and better treatment.

What Are You Speaking Up About?

You are going to tell this person that you are fed up with the toxic relationship, that you want to be treated better, that your self-worth is crucial to you and that you are not impressed by their portrayal of grandeur which makes them seem like they are larger than life.

In addition to these comments, express your peculiar experiences with the person thus far and show how their character has done more harm than good to your mental health and the relationship. The narcissist needs to understand the fact that you may be making a severe decision soon to step away from the relationship, and these are your reasons.

Don't be emotional with this step; don't cry or speak with fear, be firm and resolute in saying your piece, as this is the only way he can take you seriously. Also, reflect on real incidents between the two of you that back up your claim; this way, the narcissist wouldn't have anything to disagree with.

Remember that the fact that you are told to speak up doesn't mean you should orchestrate an attack on the narcissist; the last thing we want is to correct someone else and use the methods they use (which we hate) to do that.

You can be firm and serious about what you are saying while solely concentrating on repulsive character traits rather than the individual's skills (maybe work skills). Some people could be a narcissist and still be good at their jobs or work, so try to separate both factors when speaking out.

If the narcissist you are dealing with is a superior such as your boss in the office, you should walk up to him and express yourself politely yet firmly. In a work environment, you don't know what reaction you will get, so you will have to hope for the best. Regardless of that, you need to speak up.

✓ BUILD A SUPPORT SYSTEM

When you are near a narcissist who seems to have a lot of control, it is easy for you to ultimately make that person the object of your utmost attention and affection, which also means that you will shut other people in your life out.

Now the more the person dominates you, the more isolated you become, which means that you may not have people to share your pain with or people who will understand what you are going through and be there for you.

To handle this situation, you will have to build healthier relationships, and a support network made up of people who care about you. If you continue to spend time in a dysfunctional relationship with this person that has a narcissistic personality, you will be emotionally drained.

We all need a support system made up of people who believe in us and cheer us on to greatness; we need a support system of people who trust us and those who are concerned about our well-being. A support system also serves as the pillar in our lives that hold us together when it seems like we are about to break down.

Try to rekindle old friendships while nurturing new ones, get together with your family often, and explore new places with people who value your opinion and love having you around them. Get active in your community, as this will enable you to meet people who are as passionate as you are about specific issues.

When you build a support system and rely on it, you will understand that you have been doing so much harm to yourself by staying with a narcissist. You will also get to see how brightly your personality shines amid people you are comfortable with.

Make up for the nights you couldn't hang out with your friends because the narcissist in your life made it imperative for you to choose him over your pals. When you do get out of the grasp of the narcissist, that is when you realize how exciting the world is and how much you can have in an uplifting environment.

If you work for a narcissistic boss who makes you stay up late in the office even when you could do the work the following day, you must find a way to leave the office at the agreed time on your contract.

If you isolated yourself in the past because of a narcissistic relationship, it is time to rebuild your support system; it is time to reach out to those who know the value of your voice and those who see you as a blessing to their lives.

You have spent so much time seeing yourself through the eyes of a narcissist; it is time to see yourself bloom in the eyes of others and accept your uniqueness while basking in your strength. When you have your support system, you won't need to rely entirely on the narcissist for emotional support, and you will be mentally protected from the abuse inflicted on you.

✓ DON'T GIVE IN TO DEMANDS OR MANIPULATION

When a narcissist observes that he no longer has such a strong hold over you as he did in the past, he will resort to manipulation or start making demands of you to get your attention again.

Most narcissists resort to this approach when it seems like they are losing the empathic person because now there is no one else to tolerate their excessive behavior. Some people give in to narcissists' manipulations, and just like that, they are right back to where they started.

But you know this now, and you ought to be prepared. Don't give in to manipulation from a narcissist; make sure you stand your ground when it comes to insisting on what is right for you. In some extreme cases, the narcissist may end up crying, screaming, throwing a tantrum, or doing several other things to strong-arm you into being at their mercy again.

At this point, you must show your resilience and determination by putting your foot down and insisting on a changed behavior or nothing at all. Listen, narcissists are naturally manipulative people, it's just what they do, and you are not wired that way, so in a battle over manipulation, you will not win.

This means that you must rely on your empathic strength by realizing that staying away from a narcissist is a way of expressing kindness to yourself long-term.

The narcissist can also start to make demands that he knows you can never meet to get your attention, and if you give in to such requests, you will be handing over power to this person all over again.

This is the time when you need to show authority and power with your character. You don't have to talk so much or try to convince the narcissist that he has a problem and that is the reason for your actions. This is not the phase to try and discuss anything because you already know who you are dealing with, and you are set to get out.

When the narcissist makes unreasonable demands, shut them down with a stalwart refusal; don't be mild or meek about it because he will be searching for a weak spot to hammer on, and you cannot afford the luxury of being vulnerable right now.

You will know you are being manipulated when you divert from "handling" the situation to "tolerating" it; you will also see that manipulation has set in when you no longer feel the need to insist on what is right in the relationship.

Manipulation wouldn't happen at once; it starts to creep in subtly and eventually gets the better of you. At such moments, you need to go back and think about why you started on this journey toward handling the situation.

Make it clear that you will accept nothing less than a complete reformation in character while outlining everything you will require in the relationship going forward. Narcissists tend to believe that manipulation works primarily if they got their way in the past, so you must understand that you are at a pivotal point now where you can change the narrative entirely for the individual.

Your emotional state going forward now is your responsibility, and giving in to the narcissist will be problematic for your mental and physical health.

✓ *INSIST ON THE ACTION, NOT PROMISES*

When the narcissist sees that you are holding on to your claims and you are not willing to compromise even in the face of pressing demands and manipulation, he will resort to making promises to change.

You should understand that not all narcissists give up on bending the other person to his will, and the changes we are anticipating that will lead to the narcissist making promises might not happen immediately.

Some narcissists might be way more difficult to handle, which means that your determination to get it down must be stronger than their commitment to continually hold on to you.

However, when they do start to feel the pressure from your new behavior, they will give in by making promises to you; in fact, at such moments, you will think you are dealing with a different person entirely because they will be so desperate to get your attention back.

So, the promises will roll in, but you must be very careful and not get carried away by the idea of getting signs from this person that robbed you of so many experiences. The narcissist may promise to do better, change, become more conscious of your emotions, or even keep you at the center of the relationship.

You should know this will be a ploy to get you right back to the relationship, and narcissists are good at making promises; they tend to promise to do whatever you want them to do and say they will be better. In some cases, the narcissist might be sincere about making changes, but these promises are just a means to an end.

The motivation to be better will be lost when you give the narcissist what he wants. If the narcissist is very smart, he will attempt to be better in the first few days so you will believe in the effort being made, but this change will not be sustained.

✓ DON'T GIVE IN WHEN PROMISES ARE MADE; INSIST ON THE ACTION!

Promises are a probability, they are words that are spoken to secure the moment, and they can be broken at any time (a narcissist doesn't consider the value of a promise). So, insist on actions that back up the hopes and don't make changes until you get what you want.

Request the changes you seek, stand your ground, and insist that you will only fulfill their application after they have fulfilled yours. To make things even more serious, tell them to share ideas with you on how they intend to start implementing the change. Do they intend to sign up for therapy, speak with friends, or have moments of personal reflection? What exactly do they want to do that will bring about "change?" The answers you will get from the individual will ascertain if their promises are real or if they don't intend to do anything about it.

Now, if the narcissist tells you that they will work on it, it isn't good enough. Nothing is as good as action at this moment; they must be seen doing before you can consider going back.

But even after taking a step toward fulfilling his promise, you must make sure there is a consistency of action. Of course, you don't have to force the person to become consistent, but you must monitor the progress.

So, there are three strands to this step:

Promise = Action = Consistency

A promise from a narcissist might be a verbal affirmation of what they might do, but if they are not inspired by anything, in particular, they would rather not take action at all.

However, when they find a good reason to take action, they will; this is where the real challenge lies. Most narcissists find it difficult to embrace the empathic side of life (it's just not in their nature, but it doesn't mean that it is impossible).

For some, they begin and cannot make it through to the end, so the action aspect is where you would have to monitor and insist on the action because there is a higher chance of this person making it through to the end if they make it halfway.

Consistency is hard for narcissists because they live in whatever moment feeds their ego, so they may give a promise, take action for a while and not be consistent with it. If they are not consistent, then there are no guarantees that they are learning anything.

So, if you find out that they are making progress from the therapist or whoever they are working with to get better, you must make sure there is some improvement with the results before going back (if you ever do).

Some narcissists stop at the first strand by just making a promise, others stop at the second strand by taking action and only a few remain consistent with the changes. If you must stay with that person, then he must complete all three strands!

✓ OFFER HELP

If you sense that the narcissist truly wants to change but doesn't know how to go about it, you can offer to help. Now, by offering help, we are not saying you should go all out, abandon your life and take on the growth of this individual.

Some narcissists may be passionate about change after watching you insist on it, but they may not know where to start, so you can offer advice and suggestions on what you think they should do first or how they should commence the process.

The first step of helping them you can utilize is to show them what empathy feels like, you are an empathic person, and you have shown that it is one of the most influential personality traits a person can embody. So, teach this narcissist with your character, show him through your words and actions that it is okay to be humane, patient, emotionally available, and aware of how others feel.

You can also help a narcissist get help by recommending that they seek professional help with a therapist; sometimes, the narcissist needs to open up to someone else (a third party) by sharing how they feel and learning how to develop their emotional balance. Therapy sessions will also enhance the narcissist's communicative abilities, which will add some value to his relationship-building abilities.

Another suggestion that will help the narcissist is to seek out the people in his life that may have been affected by their character and get them to share their experiences with him. We often do not believe what people say about us until we listen.

In this case, the narcissist will be getting real-life proof from those around him in the form of their stories. Your job is to inform these people of your decision and then persuade them to help out as well by being truthful and honest with the narcissist.

When recommending ways for narcissists to seek help, try not to impose your suggestions because this might cause the individual to become aggressive because a narcissist doesn't want to be controlled. So, your role in helping him get help should be strictly on a voluntary basis.

You need to monitor from afar and ascertain if they are sticking to the plan or taking the process of change seriously. Now when you notice a pattern of non-compliance, there is only one thing you can do: Walk away without a second thought!

✓ *WALK AWAY*

Finally, when and if all else fails, you will have to step away from the relationship and no turning back. Of course, this step is the last resort when you realize that everything else has not worked, but it is also a harrowing one if you ever get to this point.

As much as no one wants to be in a relationship with a narcissist, you will agree that if the person has been in your life for a long time, you will feel that initial reluctance not to want to let go, but, trust me, you must!

Walking away from such a relationship doesn't mean you failed, it simply means you did your best, but this other person wasn't willing to pick up the slack and you cannot afford to sit around waiting for him to do something when it is convenient.

Most of the time, people who are emotionally affected by narcissists find it challenging to walk away; especially if it's an empathic person, there will always be that desire to wish for the best and hope that it will all work out eventually. But don't forget that that is what the narcissist is counting on.

But here's a newsflash, nothing works out by itself; you've got to do something for results to manifest, and if the person in question isn't willing to take action, then it is okay to walk away.

The narcissist puts himself first all of the time, regardless of how anyone else feels, so it really wouldn't be a problem if you do the same for yourself at this point. You have done well by recommending help and taking on the other redemptive steps proffered, so you need to put yourself first now because if you don't walk away, you will continually experience emotional suppression and every different negative feeling that a narcissist enables.

If you struggle with the thought of walking away even after doing everything you could to handle the situation, then you need to take time off to reflect on your life and ask yourself specific questions, which include:

- Am I happy in this relationship?
- Do I feel fulfilled with this individual?
- Does this person make me feel safe?
- Am I my true and authentic self whenever I am around this person?

The answers you get from the questions above will prompt you to take this step because in the end if you are not happy, then maybe it's time to move on. The reasons for walking away from a narcissist vary based on the type of relationships formed (for example, if you had a narcissistic boss and you love your job, you might experience conflict within yourself, wondering if you should walk away from the job or if you should stay). Now for that decision, you will have to take a stand without interference from anyone else because you know the extent of your love for the job and your experiences with the boss.

If it is a job, you can walk away from, then do it with your head held up high because you are valuable; on the other hand, if you choose to stay, then you must be able to build up emotional resistance that will protect you from the hurtful words and expressions you will continue to endure with this narcissist.

The choice is always yours, but after all, is said and done, no one should have to remain in an abusive or toxic relationship. Make all the effort you can and do your best, but if there are no sustainable changes, you must walk away if it doesn't work.

The people in our lives who matter to us must realize when they have a problem and know how to deal with it; making excuses for them may be portrayed as an act of love, but it isn't.

✓ *ACCEPT YOURSELF*

Fighting nature is not only futile, but it can be disastrous. You can't pretend you don't have feelings, and you can't deny that you sense what others feel. You can't lock yourself inside and never allow experiences to come into your life. These characteristics are what define you as an empath.

The best thing to do for yourself, and those around you, is to accept yourself as you are. Social standards and your heightened sense of emotional sensitivity might not agree with you, and some people may find you too much. But that's OK. You likely find the "average" person too much for you as an empath.

Accepting yourself at your best and your worst is one of the most powerful things you can do for your mental and physical health. It is, in fact, the first step to make towards managing the downsides of being an empath and learning how to live in a balanced way.

Look at yourself and analyze what you see. How are you defined? Which parts, habits, and traits of you are you proud of? How can you improve the ones you are ashamed of? In truth, it might feel uncomfortable at first, and you may want to just think about good things. Try to fight that. Look at yourself in the mirror and figuratively strip down to your soul and accept what you see in all its splendor and uniqueness with the same human compassion you show others so frequently.

✓ TRUST YOURSELF

It is okay to doubt yourself from time to time. We all have a tiny critic in our head who doubts every decision that we make. Self-doubt can creep in easily. As an empath, you might tend to make space within yourself for the energy and opinions of others. Therefore, the opinion that is the most dominant will rule the roost. It might make you start questioning your decision. Usually, when this happens, empaths tend to talk themselves out of their true feelings or intuition. Even if they are the quiet ones, empaths are naturally quite perceptive and intuitive. This means that they are often right. Even so, some are among the first to assume they are wrong. This is one of the paradoxes of being an empath.

It is okay to take some time and even question yourself. Self-reflection is a helpful tool. However, if you notice that you constantly doubt your feelings or opinions and seek constant validation from others, it is time to correct this. Keep in mind that you're the only one who knows what is right for you, no one else can determine this. Your opinions matter, they are valid, and they are real. Never let anyone else make decisions for you or try to talk you out of your feelings. It is time that you understand there exists a difference between those people who offer support and reflection and those who encourage self-doubt. Start trusting yourself before believing others' opinions about you. Here is a simple exercise you can follow for self-evaluation.

Close your eyes, relax your body and concentrate on your breathing. With every breath that you take, visualize that you fill in your body with positive energy. As you exhale, visualize that all self-doubt is slowly expelled from your body. Do this for a while until all the feeling of self-doubt or a lack of trust leaves your body. If you're struggling with pushing these feelings out, you can try saying them out loud, visualize them as they're leaving your tongue and your teeth, and look at them as they dissolve in the air like a cloud. Push all self-doubt away. Keep doing this for as long as you need, and get rid of all insecurities. As you do this, you will start to feel lighter and better. Start embracing your intuition. How does this feel? The more you tune into your intuition, the more you will be filled with self-belief. You can also repeat certain affirmations like "I trust myself," "I fully trust my intuition and my instinct," and "I validate my feelings and they are important." You might not always get answers immediately after doing this exercise, but it will certainly give you some clarity. Once your mind is free from self-doubt, your intuition will shine bright.

You can practice this exercise whenever you feel you're starting to doubt yourself. You can also do this whenever you feel stressed or anxious.

✓ LOVE YOURSELF

You must learn to love yourself. It is okay to place yourself before others. As an empath, you might tend to feel guilty whenever you do this. Well, it is time to rest all those misconceptions. You don't have to feel guilty for doing what's best for you. Don't think that this makes you selfish or uncaring. Only when you can function at your best will you be able to help others. You must make it a daily habit of doing something that you truly enjoy and love. It can be something as simple as taking a moment to pause, close your eyes and take a breath of fresh air. Appreciate the beauty of nature, the gentle breeze blowing around you, or even play with your pet. Do something that is just for yourself and no one else. Taking a couple of momentary pauses every day will help you become more mindful of your present and also get in touch with your inner child. There are different ways in which you can take care of yourself like going on a long walk, painting, writing, drawing, taking a leisurely bath, spending time with your loved ones, meditating, or even listening to music. You can pretty much do anything that makes you happy. Maybe you can take up an old hobby of yours or even learn something new. Essentially, it is about doing things that make you feel better about yourself.

✓ *SET UP BOUNDARIES*

Empaths find it tough to set boundaries because they don't like to hurt, upset, or offend anyone.

You spend a great deal of energy worrying about situations. Even if you have a desire to set boundaries, you quickly back out because of guilty feelings. To the empath, saying "no" feels like a dagger through the heart because they feel responsible for that person's emotional well-being, so you spend most of your life trying to avoid this.

You have perfected this avoidance technique, but the truth is that you are doing more harm than good. When you don't set boundaries from the start, you allow other people's negative circumstances into your life, which will ultimately lead to your downfall. Before we learn how to set boundaries, let's look at what they entail.

❖ What Are Boundaries?

A boundary is an invisible line that separates two people. Boundaries put distance between your needs, feelings, and responsibilities and the responsibilities of others. The boundaries you set tell people what behavior you find acceptable and unacceptable, and how you will allow them to treat you. People who don't set boundaries are often taken advantage of. They are what I have termed "yes-yes people," your wish is their command, they can never say no.

Why Do Empaths Need Boundaries?

Boundaries Protect You

One of the many advantages of being an empath is that you can feel other people's emotions. So, you know when negative energy is about to invade your space. When you set boundaries, you keep out the energy vampires who are constantly draining you of your time and emotions.

Boundaries Show You Value Yourself

"Yes-yes people" are very insecure, whether this is a conscious or unconscious behavior, they are constantly seeking validation from others, which is one of the reasons they find it so difficult to say no. Empaths often believe they are responsible for how other people feel because they can pick up on it so easily. The truth is, you are only responsible for how you feel, and when you set emotional boundaries, it shows that you are not willing to allow people to take advantage of you.

Boundaries also keep you from burning yourself out—you can't take part in everything. There will be social events, committee meetings, and projects that you will have to say no to. Your priorities should come first and not everybody else's.

Boundaries Allow You to be True to Yourself

People who don't set boundaries constantly have people in their space, even if they don't want them there. When you don't have time to yourself, you can't be yourself because you are either trying to impress someone or cater to their needs, which is not a good place to be. You need to spend time alone to make your own decisions, process your feelings, and meet your needs.

Why Do You Find It Difficult to Set Boundaries?

There are some deep-rooted issues that you may not be aware of that prevent you from setting boundaries in your life.

- **Low self-esteem**: Even though you have all these magnificent powers, empaths are often very insecure. Not only do they have to deal with a weird gift that they feel no one understands, but it also leads them to seek approval from others. Empaths want to feel normal. They don't like feeling like a freak of nature and acceptance from others gives them that feeling. So, empaths tend to put others before themselves. This might sound like a selfless Gandhi-type altruistic act, but it becomes a problem when you are doing it for approval.

- **Fear**: Setting boundaries is not normal for empaths, as they are constantly allowing people to overstep the mark because they don't like upsetting people. Not only are they afraid of absorbing the other person's negative energy when they say no, but empaths are also afraid of the rejection that may come with turning people down.

- **You don't know how to set boundaries**: Some people simply don't know how to set boundaries. You may have grown up in a household where boundaries were not set, and so it has become the norm for you. The good news is that you can learn how to set boundaries.

- **People-pleasing**: Empaths don't like conflict, and they would rather say yes to something that upsets someone by saying no, even if it will be inconvenient.

Overcoming the Fear of Creating Boundaries

So, you know what? YOU NEED BOUNDARIES! Especially if not only do you want to survive but you want to thrive as an effective empath. And you are going to have to get used to setting them. As I'm sure you already know, people are attracted to your energy and want to be around you constantly, so you are going to have to get used to setting boundaries. Here are some tips to help you overcome this fear:

- **It's a healthy form of self-love**. Everyone has needs and that includes you. Sometimes, you just need space to take care of yourself; there is nothing wrong with that. Ask yourself this: do you feel guilty about eating more fruits or vegetables? You are probably staring at the page right now, thinking, "What a dumb question!" Well, in the same way, eating more fruits and vegetables is good for the body, so setting boundaries is good for your emotional health. Why should you feel guilty about setting boundaries if you wouldn't feel guilty for eating a healthy diet?

- **Get to know yourself**. If you don't spend any time alone, you will never truly know who you are. It's practically impossible to set boundaries if you are so consumed with what everyone else needs that you don't know what you need. Spend time tuning into your feelings and thoughts. Take time out throughout the day to ask yourself, "What do I need?" and "How do I feel?" When you understand your wants and needs better, you will find it easier to set boundaries.

- **You are not a therapist**. And even if you were, the friends who call you every second of the day are not paying for your services. It may be that with all the problems they seem to have, they might actually need some professional help. And that may be good advice to give.

- **Setting boundaries benefit everyone.** Setting boundaries doesn't just benefit you, it's also good for everyone around you. When everyone understands where they stand in the relationship, it makes life a whole lot easier. Have you ever just snapped at someone for no apparent reason? Most people are going to answer yes to this question because one of the consequences of not setting boundaries is never saying how you really feel and then snapping.

❖ 3 Rules To Be Happy As An Empath

1. Time by Yourself to Recharge

Empaths are loving and compassionate people. They give more than they get and sometimes find themselves drained. Empaths need time by themselves to recharge, especially if they are surrounded by negativity. This is the only way they can be the best version of themselves for others.

2. Avoid Meaningless Small Talk, In Favor of Deep and Meaningful Conversations

Empaths should avoid meaningless small talk and prefer having deep and meaningful conversations with others. Small talk is the type of conversation that is not connected to feelings, beliefs, or values and deals with topics like the weather or work gossip. It's often used as filler for silence, and it can be tiresome for people to constantly "keep up" with their work culture.

Empaths who enjoy small talk may want to limit their exposure to retain a healthy aura because smaller emotions can affect empaths faster than larger ones (in the same way that an odor affects your sense of smell more quickly than it would your taste buds). Empaths are also vulnerable on an energetic level when they are exposed to this type of conversation. Small talk can also make a person feel resentful and angry because they only get a fraction of the real meaning from the information they come across in these conversations.

Empaths should initially also try to limit their use of humor in small talk. Humor is a good way to make a socially smart and good impression, but it can be very off-putting if you don't know what the other person's sense of humor is all about. This is because an indirect message can get disguised between the lines, there is a high chance of double-entendres, and you may not pick up on the original meaning behind it, which could cause feelings to be hurt. Humor, irony and sarcasm are to be used as you are sure you understand the person's values and vulnerabilities.

Highly sensitive empaths should also try to avoid public gatherings in which they feel exposed. If an empath feels uncomfortable in a certain setting, it can affect their aura and leave them feeling tense and irritated, whereas they might be able to cope with other settings better. Empaths should also be aware that conversations can quickly turn into gossip, which may aggravate them and make them feel ill at ease.

When people start small talk with you, it doesn't mean they are being unfriendly or threatening. They may just want to share something about themselves with you as an interest or they may be trying to make conversation with you because it is important to them, or they require attention.

Finally, empaths should beware and avoid being around people who constantly disagree with them. This can leave them confused and upset because they may find it difficult to understand why someone would want to be hostile toward them. It's hard for empaths to understand why anyone would be so negative about something so simple, and this can result in frustration.

3. Cut Off Energy Vampires

Empaths are often told to "develop a tough skin" or "not take things so personally," but that advice is about as helpful as telling someone who is struggling with depression to cheer up. Empaths are walking wound collectors because they feel everything—as do energy vampires. Energy vampires feed off the empathy's negativity, and this abuse may lead an empath into depression. If you're an empath, you can help prevent further abuse from energy vampires by developing what's called a "shield." A shield is a visualization of an orb or dome in front of your body that only allows positive energies to enter and block out negative energies (including thoughts).

❖ The Seven Stages To Create Your Shield

Stage 1: Recognizing the Abuse

In order to effectively combat energy vampires, you must first recognize when you are being abused. Energy vampires, especially in person, can be nearly impossible to detect. They suck out your energy without a trace to gain a physical or emotional advantage. Sometimes they don't even realize that they're doing it because this behavior is instinctive for them—it's as if you were suddenly drained of energy while sitting in front of your computer. The abuse may be subtle or blunt. It can take the form of a thought or even as a physical blow (which you'll feel, but no one else will). Think about this: If someone wants something from you and is willing to abuse you to get it, would that make them an energy vampire? That's right. Take away what they want, take away what they're doing to get it and the energy vampire will lose their reason for being.

Make sure to guard yourself against a vampire by recognizing the warning signs that you are being abused. If you feel drained after a short interaction with someone, that's probably an energy vampire. This is likely an energy vampire if you are a target just because of your personality rather than what you've accommodated in the past. If someone takes something out of their life just because they want it and then bursts into tears later when they realize they're not getting what they wanted, this is definitely an energy vampire. There are many other ways in which an abuser communicates their disregard for you and your well-being to others (like being rude or emotionally abusive). To further cement this, an abuser is always trying to control you or make you feel small. These are all signs that you may be dealing with energy vampires who, because they are lacking in self-confidence, will try to feed from your energy and attention.

Stage 2: Recognizing the Vampire

Once you have a good idea of what exactly is happening to you and have a general idea of how the energy vampire operates, it's time to take action. Remember that they're more likely to "turn" on the moment when there's a benefit (in other words, he/she/they like being in your life for the benefits rather than the sacrifices).

The next step is looking for ways to identify the energy vampires in your environment. Being mindful of the people who stop by or send you messages may be helpful. For instance, are you receiving emails from someone that are filled with negativism? They're probably coming from an energy vampire. Are they asking for money? Well, it's not likely that a genuine human being would be asking for money like that; it's more likely these emails come from a place of desperation and could possibly be written by an energy vampire as well (especially if they're scammers).

You can also look for other signs indicating that an individual could be a vampire.

Look for signs of low self-confidence, poor boundaries and no sense of personal pride. It's also common to see people acting out against those around them to get their way, which is a sign that they're not in control of their lives. In fact, it's likely that even when they are controlling others, they are just going through the motions and aren't happy or "in charge," so to say. They like being in control and will act out against people until they find someone who can accept it (which usually happens when you're younger).

But what's most important is that you take action. These people see people with strong self-confidence and a good sense of self-worth as threats—so you need to protect yourself (just like from any other predator).

Stage 3: The Shield

Now it's time to create your shield. Remember, the only way to effectively deal with an energy vampire is to create a barrier between them and yourself. This barrier has several layers of protection, so you'll want to be careful about how you create your shield. Try not to surround yourself with multiple energy vampires at once. Each person has their own frequency, and if you surround yourself with too many people that are draining, likely, your shield will not be strong enough.

In order to create your shield, you must first build the foundation of power within you. Start by breathing in deeply and picturing yourself in a place where you feel safe and happy: This can be anywhere—as long as it makes you feel comfortable. Now focus on reaching down into your core and pulling power from within. Then imagine this energy coursing around your body like a flood of blue light (this is because blue represents peace, which is what the empath needs). This blue light will start at your feet and slowly work its way up to the top of your head. It will also surround your heart, where your will, personality, and life force are located. Now visualize with your mind's eye an energy coming out from your chest area, flowing through your arms and hands, and forming a cupular shape of blue energy that makes you invincible. This shield creates your new confidence and self-worth, and self-love will get stronger and stronger every time you use it until it becomes your strongest defense against bad energies.

Stage 4: Find a Partner Who Understands and Embraces Your Personality

Empaths may find a partner who understands and embraces their personality and insights, but when they meet someone who reacts poorly to their hypersensitivity and energy, the problem is compounded. They are often able to sense how a partner feels about them or their needs. Finding a new love interest can be difficult if you're an empath because it's hard to figure out what makes someone tick. If you're looking for love, a way around some of these problems might be to consider dating an empath yourself!

Love is rarely perfect, but finding your match might just be worth the effort. Some of the easiest steps you can take are making sure that your potential mate has empathy and also learning about yourself so that your expectations are realistic.

1. Learn About the Empath Personality Trait

If you believe that your new love interest is an empath, it's important to learn how to recognize a person with this trait. The first step is to dispel any misconceptions and myths you may have about what it means to be an empath and what traits they will share with you. Although many people are identified as having this trait, there's no one definition of what being an empath entail. Understand that there are several levels of sensitivity and many different versions of the trait as a whole.

2. Recognize Your Own Empathy Level

It's important to recognize your own emotional responsiveness and hypersensitivity, even if you think that an empath won't be attracted to you because of it. You're not alone in experiencing strong emotions. A lot of people with this trait have a high sensitivity level, including those who are either hypersensitive or not hypersensitive enough. If you are an empath and think that someone would be more attracted to you if you "toughened up," it's time to get some insight into your kind of connection. Both individuals with empathy traits need to know what they feel and how they feel about their partners.

3. Avoid Comparing Yourself to Others

Avoid comparing your reality with what other people say about empaths. This can cause a lot of unnecessary problems and hurt feelings. You're better off exploring who you are and what you expect from your mate.

4. Know the Difference Between Empathy and Daydreaming.

While it's true that you will more likely have stronger connections with someone who has been through a similar situation, daydreaming is not the same as being an empath. It's easy to confuse the two traits because they seem similar, but they are not at all alike in personality or behavior. You might think that you're daydreaming about things that are going on in your own life, but it's important to recognize the difference between an empath who is "in their head" and someone whose mind is wandering to a place unrelated to the conversation at hand.

Stage 5: Develop Daily Mindfulness Habits

It is suggested that an empath develop daily mindfulness habits to increase their ability to read other humans and their emotions. With that in mind, here are the steps that an empath can take to develop mindfulness.

Start by sitting down and focusing on your breath for a few minutes. Breathe in deeply and slowly, breathing out completely before inhaling again. The objective is to focus on a single sensation of your breath, such as the air filling your lungs or moving all around you when you exhale.

Focus on your posture and how it feels throughout the day while staying aware of what you're feeling in general. Pay attention to whether you're feeling irritated or happy, and focus on your physical body as best as you can.

Pay attention to your emotions as they happen instead of allowing yourself to react in your habitual way. When you have an emotion, do not force it into thinking about what the emotion means or what it will do.

Instead, try to observe the sensation for a few minutes until it passes without causing you any problems.

Notice that feelings often come one after another. Watch them for a while before they pass on their own accord or when they somehow end themselves when they reach an unbalanced stage that is difficult to maintain. Watching emotions rise and fall in your mind can be enlightening.

Learn to gradually let go of negative feelings when they arise and slowly allow a more positive feeling to take control. A good example of this is letting go of anger by envisioning something soothing or calming, something from your past, present or future. Envision a completely calm and peaceful scene while you meditate. With practice, these visualizations will help you drop negative emotions little by little. I suggest you to visualize happy memories or think about something positive whenever possible, even during your daily routine. This will help you to gradually get used to letting go of negative emotions and help you become more calm and more collected.

Learn to use your personal mindfulness when you experience negative emotions from the past. For example, when being angry, try to imagine the person that caused your anger, where he's coming from, all the burdens he had to go through that led you to feel that way; and think that you understand this person and you are above him, in your reign of calmness. Imagine floating up toward the sky, leaving your old negative feeling on the ground level. Watch him and your feelings - they are not you - and smile. This may seem silly at first, but it can help your anger and negative emotions are about to take control of you in the present.

As you become more aware of the tools of your mind, you will develop your natural intuition and how to deal with people and situations. This skill is extremely important for empaths, as it will help you feel more in control of your emotions and how you act around others.

Stage 6: Find a Comfortable and Stimulating Workplace

Empaths should find a comfortable and stimulating work environment. Some natural light is good, but not too much. A quiet office where the conversation is not permitted can be very disheartening and harmful to your mental well-being. Light and occasional murmuring can give you the "white noise" to help you focus. Additionally, the space must suit you: a large open room with lots of windows would be too much light for someone who suffers from Seasonal Affective Disorder, or SAD. At the same time, a small dark room might make you claustrophobic and restless. Remember that an imbalance of colors may also be distracting, leading to eye fatigue or headaches throughout the day. It is best to find your right balance of light and dark, as well as a variety of colors so that you can sit anywhere in the office without feeling like you are missing out on something.

Lack of sleep and depression are often issues in empaths. The empath is highly sensitive to the natural energy waves that surround us all. When this sensitivity is not properly managed, it can cause an imbalance in energy that increases depression and fatigue. There are ways for you to manage this issue, and many people use healing crystals to help themselves feel better.

Empaths are people who tend to feel things more keenly than others. They tend to absorb other people's emotions and sometimes, in a workplace, this can be overwhelming. Their feelings are so intense that they can not only feel others' pain but even physical disease. If you are working in an office with other people, here the shielding techniques are vital for your job and your life. I invite you to not only imagining a shield, but to bring it to the next level: make your shield evolve in a bubble that will work as an armor for whatever psychic attack you might receive from the external world. Everything that approaches your bubble is either 1) Eliminated or 2) Falls in line to get processed and evaluated by you. Is it worth your attention? Good, then you deal with it.

If you don't do this by taking on the emotions of others, empaths may often experience emotional chaos in their daily working lives. Empaths end up feeling like no one else understands them because they don't know how to communicate what they are feeling to their colleagues in a way that can be understood by those who have not experienced being an empath.

Empaths are here on earth to serve as emotional mirrors for everyone and everything that exists here. They are here to reflect back to us our own emotions and thus awaken within us our full potential. Empaths have a great capacity for understanding, compassion, empathy, laughter, and creativity. Their ability to work in harmony with others on a spiritual level is phenomenal. However, the negative energy generated by the emotional chaos caused by those around them can make it very difficult for empaths to function on a day-to-day basis. Thus, an empath needs to learn how to manage confusing emotions so that normalcy and efficiency can be restored.

Stage 7: Be Grateful for Your Gift

Empaths should be grateful for their gift of emotional sensitivity.

Realize you are precious. Empaths are incredible beings with an incredible gift to feel and sense some of the people's most private things and emotions. Empaths have a very real but different way of perceiving the world.

A true empath is born with an innate ability to feel what another person is feeling to anticipate their needs and help them heal or give them comfort. This gift also comes with a price, as being able to sense the emotions of others can be draining on an empath's energy levels if not handled properly or if there are too many strong negative feelings happening around them at once. In a way, an empath is also a gift to the world.

Empaths can also have experiences called "psychic attacks" that they're most likely unaware of until they've been exposed to a very powerful trauma, and then it hits them. This often results in the empath feeling weak, worthless, nauseous, or experiencing a combination of the two. That is why if you know someone who is an empath, you must protect them, especially if they're unaware of what it takes to be one.

Empaths are people who are deeply connected with their surroundings and oftentimes find themselves drawn to receiving or giving comfort to others. This doesn't mean that they're compassionate or warm to everyone they meet though. Feeling someone's emotions doesn't mean liking them, obviously, empathy is very different from sympathy.

Whether she likes it or not, the empath perceives the emotions and sensations of others, and this can be exhausting for them, especially if sustained for too long. But the other side of this is that some empath's gifts are as close as one could define psychic.

It is important to know that there's a difference between empaths and psychics, although some traits are finely correlated. Psychics (sometimes called clairsentients) can sense energy fields and in some cases, vaguer things like emotions and intentions. Empaths, on the other hand, can assume another person's identity and feel as if they are experiencing those emotions for themselves. I have written another book about it (*Empath and Psychic Abilities*, you can grab a copy here https://www.amazon.com/dp/B09P44G6K3).

On an average day, an empath can sense what's happening in the room with one look at her surroundings. In this situation, they might be hesitant to approach anyone because they're too busy sensing the room. This can look awkward for those watched, but it needs to be clear that empaths are not judging others; they simply feel other people's energy as if it were their own.

Codependent No More: *Your New Life*

For those unfamiliar with it, the word "codependency" may sound like a positive term, which may refer to something mutually beneficial. Of course, codependency refers to something "mutual," but the "beneficial" part is completely off.

The truth is, there is nothing beneficial in a codependent relationship, and neither is there anything beneficial for a codependent person. Indeed, a codependent person is someone whose relationship with himself or herself is in a state of deep-seated self-doubt, whereby they or no longer trust themselves. This may be sustainable—yet unhealthy—up to the moment when a codependent relationship ends, as at least one of the partners is likely to drown in self-abuse, self-blame, self-shaming, and an inability to handle even the slightest form of criticism. This is usually a precursor to self-sabotaging and can get as far as suicidal behaviors.

Codependency, in its basic form, is excessive psychological or emotional reliance on another person who needs support because of an addiction or ill health. A codependent person is someone who allows another person's behavior to influence them significantly to the point of taking full responsibility for controlling the other person's behavior. The codependent person enables the dependent person in the relationship. That is to say, the codependent partner behaves in ways that encourage the other partner to continue in their irresponsibility, immaturity, addiction, and illness.

Codependency goes beyond mere clinginess. A codependent person typically lives their life for their partner—their world revolves around the partner's world. They go to extreme lengths to please their partner. A codependent relationship is one in which one partner believes their sense of purpose depends on the support given to the other person, and the other person believes they need to be needed. The codependent partner usually engages in self-sacrificing behavior for the sake of their partner who, incidentally, expects nothing less. The neediness of one partner and the need to feel needed by the other partner is known as the cycle of codependency.

Codependency is not restricted to romantic partners alone. It can happen between friends, family, and even colleagues at work too. In many cases, the relationship can degenerate into a physically and emotionally abusive one. Often, other people outside the relationship can easily see that something is off, but the codependent partner usually doesn't realize it.

Road to Recovery

While codependency is a very challenging behavioral pathology, the good news is that it is definitely something that one can heal and transcend. Doing this requires a strong commitment to change one's patterns of thinking and action, hard work and a dependable support system. To make lasting changes, you must realize that the healing process is ongoing—you will likely never reach a place where you are perfect and have no more need for improvement. However, with a sincere commitment and consistent efforts, you will soon see drastic improvements immediately, leading to a healthier and happier life.

While the road to recovery is in no way easy, it offers profound rewards and has the power to free you from much unnecessary suffering, fear, and unhappiness that you had taken to be an ordinary part of life. The truth is that codependent ways of living are not necessary and not inevitable. As you change your innermost patterns and false beliefs, you may find a new life opening up for you and your close relationships.

If you happen to be in one of such relationships, three is a process called "Codependency Addiction Recovery" to work toward stopping the cycle of codependency. It may seem daunting, but it is very possible. There are countless steps you can take if you decide to take the initiative, but here I'll sum up the most effective measures you can take to recover from codependency.

Reality Check

The first thing you absolutely have to take is to look at your reality and your situation with a realistic lens. Denial is one of the most horrible enemies of healing and recovery, so sit yourself down and survey your situation and your relationship without sugarcoating anything. Knowing all aspects of a problem is the first step towards solving it, so do so with care. Even though it may be difficult, know that you are about to begin a journey of healing and recovery.

While you analyze your situation, it is also important that you avoid blaming yourself for what's happened in the past. Commit to thinking rationally and avoid as much as possible focusing on depotentiation feelings like regret, or things you should have done differently.

Acceptance

Aside from giving yourself a reality check, you also need to accept the path that brought you here and what you have come to realize about your situation. As with the previous point, denial can only serve to bring you harm. Therefore, the next step you need to take is to accept what has happened to you and to decide how you can move on for the better. Consider all the crossroads you went through and led you in your present. Understand your past self; do not make any excuse for her, but recognize the weakness and the needs of that person, who was just not ready yet to be the person that would have taken a different decision.

Recognize Your Role

Though it may be easy to blame your partner for everything that went wrong in your relationship, this is often not the case. It's also vital now that you recognize what you could have done differently if only you were stronger, and what weaknesses prevented you from breaking free of codependency. Doing so doesn't mean that you should now start self-blame. Recognizing your role simply means that you identify what aspects of yourself you can improve upon to strengthen things that can help you avoid falling back into bad habits and relationships once more.

Internal Vs. External

One important factor that you need to realize is that recovery from codependence is mostly an internal process. Before taking any additional steps, you need to realize that you need to focus internally rather than looking to external sources or other people to "fix" you. Recovering from codependency means recovering yourself; your values, your needs, your feelings, your wants, and your own identity. These can only come from within.

What are your values? Think about the person you want to become, the person that is a whole on her own that wouldn't need somebody else to be complete but it would need another glorious human being to thrive and shine even more!

Decide that from now on, you will act only moved by your values, not what feels urgent, but by what is important for you to become that person.

See the Positive

A recent study has shown that showing gratitude can actually make a person happier and more content. Though your past may be negative or hurtful, you must try and identify the aspects of your life you can be grateful for. This will help you remain positive and will help give you a perspective that not everything in your life is damaged. There is constantly something to hope for, and finding these things in your life can help you greatly on your road to rebirth.

Bad things happen, it's in the evolutionary nature of reality, and we can't avoid it. But what you and I can do, is to control what we believe in, take action, and focus on the optimistic side of everything.

Abstain

Much like any addiction, you need to be able to abstain from what was keeping you addicted. The same concept can be applied to codependency. It's important that one of the steps you take is to make yourself maintain some distance from your partner or the person that is weighing you down.

Allow yourself to enjoy a little moment of independence. Take a walk, go for a trip, or enjoy a meal at a restaurant, alone. Stand on the street and just open your arms wide, notice how much space your body occupies. Feel it.

Also, allow your partner to breathe some air without you around, as it may be helpful to them too.

Safety and Precaution

In line with the previous point, remember to take great precautions to prioritize your safety. Remember that codependent relationships can easily be abusive. If you are a victim of physical, emotional, or domestic abuse, it's vital that you first determine your "escape route" or where you can go in case of emergency.

If you feel you are at risk or in harm's way, you need to inform those close to you about what you plan to do. If and when you confront your partner, you need to make sure that you have people you can go to keep safe. This is especially important if you have children with you.

It doesn't have to go downhill, but if it does, planning ahead can save lives.

Confront Your Partner

Once you set up a safe environment, make sure that you let your partner know what you're going through. It's important that you can confront the problem you are facing; more often than not, your partner is a big part of that. Expressing yourself to a person who has kept you suppressed is not only vindicating but is also greatly freeing. It is an important step in recovery and can help you fully move from focusing on others to focusing on taking care of yourself.

Again, however, take this step with a grain of salt. If you feel that you will be putting yourself in serious danger by confronting your partner, it's important that you have people with you to remove you from the situation in case things get hostile. Make sure that the confrontation happens in a neutral place where exits are easily accessible.

This confrontation doesn't have to be a fight. You can both realize that your story has developed into an unhealthy codependent relationship.

Visualize

One of the most necessary steps in solving a problem is also knowing your goals and what you want. Therefore, it's vital to visualize yourself in a better place in terms of your relationships and your general well-being. This will also help you recover in terms of getting back to who you are and getting to know yourself again.

Don't exclusively think in terms of what you want; picture the person that you need to be in the future to get what you want instead. You just need to be her.

Challenge Negativity

A common problem that codependent people encounter is having negative thoughts about themselves. This contributes to generally impaired self-worth and keeps a person trapped in abusive situations. Therefore, challenging these negative thoughts is a vital component to recovering from codependency.

A perfect way to do this is to question and analyze whether these thoughts are grounded in reality. For example, if you begin to think that you are incompetent, ask yourself what evidence is there of your inadequacy. Did you really do anything to warrant these thoughts? Asking rational questions will help you realize that these negative thoughts are actually unfounded and that there isn't room to entertain these kinds of thoughts in daily living.

Stop The Labels

Codependent individuals often label themselves or listen to labels that other people give them. In order to battle codependency, you need to fight the urge to give yourself labels based on your mistakes or based on how others perceive you. When you find labels forming in your thoughts, consciously shift your thoughts to something more positive. Rather than calling yourself "incompetent," change this to something more constructive, like recognizing yourself as a "work in progress."

Whenever you feel the need of the simplification that a label provides, label yourself in an empowering way. Your world will reflect the words that you use to describe it.

Self-Monitor Your Progress

A necessary step in recovery is to closely monitor your own thoughts and your own self-perception. When you find yourself making mistakes or feeling down, respond with compassion rather than self-blame. Think about other times you have been challenged and the times you were able to overcome the various difficulties you've encountered. Remind yourself that you are tough and that you deserve to be free of abuse and codependency.

Self-monitoring is very useful in that you can prevent negative thoughts from escalating into more severe forms of depression or low self-esteem. Keeping a journal of your thoughts can also give you a solid record; something that you can look over to see how you've improved and to see what you need to work on even more.

Recovery can be daunting, and backsliding isn't uncommon. Therefore, you must take things to step by step. Compartmentalize and break up the recovery process into manageable tasks so as not to get overwhelmed. Set particular tasks that you need to complete in a set amount of time and write them down. Try to limit yourself to accomplishing that task within the given time, at a pace that is reasonable to you. This will help prevent frustration and will allow you time to recover in a manageable way.

Seek Professional Help

Though many victims of codependency find it difficult to approach professionals for help, know that approaching a counselor or psychologist is nothing to be ashamed of. These professionals can help you navigate the murky waters of recovery and help you sort out what has happened to you in the past. Having an objective party to talk to can also give you a special point of view; one that helps you see angles of the situation that may have been formerly unknown to you.

Just one word of advice: do not develop a codependent relationship with your counselor. I've seen this happening a couple of times. It is something to be expected, but remember that you're not the person that needs that anymore.

Celebrate Small Victories

A large part of recovering from codependency is regaining control over your life and letting the sunshine in, so to speak. A great method to do this is to celebrate the small successes and small victories that you've experienced. For example, rewarding yourself after finishing a difficult task at work may seem like a small thing, but it serves as a building block to your new foundation of self-esteem and positive self-regard. These all add up and all contribute to building a better you.

Engage in New Things

Engaging in new activities and pursuing new things will help you get back to your roots and will assist you on your journey toward self-improvement. Focus on yourself by finding out what you're good at, discovering what you enjoy, and indulging in activities that contribute to your own development. This will not only help you become better but will also help you recover from the pain of your past. A positive effect of trying out new things and mastering new skills is that these give you something that you can consider your own and can give you accomplishments that you can be proud of. Furthermore, these will help you gain a sense of independence that is much needed to combat codependency.

Pamper Yourself

Part of recovery is to indulge in your own needs and wants. Being in a codependent relationship can really exhaust you and your resources. Therefore, recovery is a time dedicated to taking care of yourself. One way to heal is to indulge and to pamper yourself by doing things that you love the most and reconnecting with what you want outside of your relationships. Remember that you don't need other people to feel good about who you are; one way to do so is to start caring for yourself rather than putting everyone else's satisfaction ahead of yours.

Reconnect

A common symptom of codependence is isolating oneself from loved ones and support networks. If you've distanced yourself from those you love and those who love you, then know that a vital step to recovery is re-establishing these ties with the people who matter most. Those who genuinely care for you will push you to be better and will encourage you to rebuild yourself no matter how challenging.

Contribute to Social Good

One great way of bolstering positivity and feeling better about life, in general, is contributing to projects of social good. Therefore, try to engage in projects and events that help others, such as a local feed the homeless program, raising donations for charities, etc.

Giving is the best way to receive; as an empath, you have a lot to give. This point is often underestimated, but those who trust this principle often find a real reason to live a life.

Give Yourself Time to Heal

Being an empath in this day and age is troublesome. The world nowadays is remorseless, cold, and fierce. Notwithstanding, it is likewise wonderful and astonishing, and the key is to never dismiss the terrific when we feel overpowered by the terrible. Not every person is an empath; obviously, however, we would all be able to use a little security from the raging battering of the world in its present manifestation.

Avoid an Excessive Number of Synthetic Substances or Sugars

Many times, being an empath implies managing overstimulation. Synthetic substances like caffeine, added substances, fake hues, and sugars can make overstimulation much more awful, prompting nervousness and different issues. Cut out the caffeine and the sugar as much as you can. If you don't have it already, you should develop a passion for all things natural.

Get Enough Rest

This appears to be an easy decision, however, what number of us really get enough rest? Not getting enough rest is frequently treated as no biggie, however, it has been demonstrated to have a similar impact on you as a .05 blood-liquor content. This dulls response times, influences exactness with errands, makes us bad-tempered, and makes things trouble us more than they should. Empaths need to have all cylinders working effectively on the off chance that we need to have the option to manage what the world is tossing at us, so make certain to get enough rest. How would you realize you've gotten enough rest? Your body will tell you. Try not to use your phone two hours before sleep, and cease any source of blue light at least half an hour before bed. As you are falling asleep, think about how good and refreshed you will feel when you wake up.

Meditate

In today's rushed world, it's hard to even think about seizing some time to stop, relax, breathe and let our minds wander. Yet, it's one of the most helpful practices we could perform, especially if we live in a chaotic city.

There is evidence that meditation can be superior to mental medications for battling uneasiness, misery, and different other issues.

It might sound tough to start, particularly with our general public's constrained abilities to focus, but if you keep it consistent, it will pay many dividends. The first time you meditate, you can last 3 minutes, it's fine. Breathe slowly and let the air out. Focus on the air as it enters and as it exits your nose and mouth. After a few times, your mind will start to feel calm, absent but fully expanded. Try to reach at least the 20-minute mark; over time, you will see a change in your energy and mental clarity.

Remember to Be Appreciative

This one isn't as simple as one may assume. Consider this: in the course of one day, how frequently do you simply feel sincere appreciation? How regularly are you appreciative of what you have, or then again only grateful for being alive? It tends to be extremely hard to recall beneficial things when we are under a consistent flood of antagonism from all sides. It's all over the place, and we can undoubtedly be pulled into despair over it on the off chance that we don't advise ourselves that there is good out there, too. Simple methods to do that can be: a search for accounts of individuals helping one another, recording five things you are thankful for consistently and saying them for all to hear, helping other people who are less lucky (appreciation is infectious!), recollecting times when you were less blessed and how life has improved... There are such a significant number of things to be thankful for in this life. Keep them in your mind.

Let Yourself Be Astounded

We underestimate numerous things in this life, however, if we truly consider them, such a significant number of them are really stunning. Everything from the tiny seeds of a strawberry to the mechanics of the human hand claims their wonders. How regularly do you consider it?

Get Back to Nature

Perhaps the main motivation individuals are so unhappy these days is that they are living lives they were not made for. People were not made to work, rest and kick the bucket. We are magnificently, flawlessly, incredibly complex enthusiastic animals equipped for a tremendous range of behavior and feeling. We live unnatural lives contrasted with our predecessors and forget to reconnect with what is extremely advantageous for the brain, body, and soul: nature. Put the telephone down. Shut down the TV. Take a walk. Go outdoors. You know what? Go shoeless! Have you ever heard about "earthing"? It's strolling barefoot on the earth, connecting directly with the ground. There is a whole science behind this, and it feels great in any case (it deals with our body's bioelectric circuits, and it's something extremely relieving for empaths to do). Get some outside air and truly allow yourself to be alive for a while. You'll be astounded by what a difference something so simple can make.

Visualize Security for Yourself

If you wind up in a circumstance that is overpowering you (such as a spot where there are a ton of others or when managing an enthusiastic vampire), the best security is in your brain. Empaths and touchy spirits get others' enthusiastic vibrations like a receiving wire. This can make being around huge gatherings of individuals troublesome and debilitating, even terrifying or alarming. The best way to win it is to prevent gathering this damaging energy. Before entering the circumstance, close your eyes and imagine the excessive energy being obstructed from you. You can envision your invincible shield or air pocket around yourself that can't get past. You can imagine an entryway shutting and blocking access to the openings of your mind, a string being unplugged, a strip being cut... Whatever image you want to conjure, you can utilize it, and it will work.

There is no incorrect method to do it. It can take some training to get it under control; however, the significant thing is that the perception is solid. If you are now in the circumstance and feel overpowered, you can either go into a quiet zone and do it or basically concentrate hard right where you are. It doesn't take long, and you should feel some discharge from the weight of others' pressure right away.

Learn to Say "No"

One thing to keep in mind: you don't owe anybody anything. Obviously, we are entrusted with helping other people; that is the reason we were made as empaths. This doesn't imply that we are expected to help other people with our own impediments. Narcissists and other passionate parasites love empaths. They search us out because we resemble clairvoyant batteries to them, and they will hold tight, depleting us until there is not all that much on the off chance that we don't stop them. Helping other people should never be a weight. Tune in to yourself and realize when that's it. And say the magic word, "No." Do it politely but firmly.

You are just figuring out how to ground and secure yourself, you are improving your life so that also those you love will take benefit in dealing with a version of you who is happy and ready to give.

Master Your Emotion and Your Thought Process

No emotion is going to be stronger than your desire for change. The moment you decide to change is the moment change happens. You start to bring about a shift in your emotions when you decide you want to turn things around. Let's talk about emotional intelligence really quickly and see how the core pillars will help you masterfully as you learn to control your anger, depression, and anxiety. The five core pillars of emotional intelligence are:

- Self-awareness
- Self-regulation
- Empathy
- Motivation
- Social skills

Improve – *5 Elements of Emotional Intelligence*

SELF-AWARENESS –
Keeping a journal
Obsere how people respond to your behavior

SELF-REGULATION –
Practice response instead of reaction.
Accepting that some things are out of control.

MOTIVATION –
Remember your "Why"
Focus on what you like about your job.

SOCIAL SKILL –
Be authentic.
Praise others and provide constructive feedback.

EMPATHY –
Avoid distractions when somebody is talking.
Understand their point of view.

Each pillar plays a specific role that is essential in changing your perception and the way you view and handle things that happen in your life. We will talk about these points in this book, but for now, just realize that masterful control through emotional intelligence happens when:

* You Develop a Greater Sense of **Self-Awareness**—By far the most important pillar out of the entire five, self-awareness is the foundation that sets the standard for the other four pillars. Particularly when it comes to conquering your emotions. Being aware of your emotions and how they affect you and the people around you is a skill that not many people have mastered because it's not as easy as it sounds. On paper, it does but put it into practice, you'll see what a challenge it can be to shift your emotions if you don't understand what it is that you're feeling.

* You Learn to **Be Assertive**—Anxiety and depression, for example, can cause many people to be wary of or afraid of their emotions. As such, they have difficulty expressing and asserting the way they feel. Emotional intelligence encourages awareness about how you feel and regulate your emotions, so you can deal with them. You are stronger than any emotion that you feel.

* **Respond Appropriately**—Responding negatively results in subsequent negative reactions, leading to anxiety, negativity, chronic worry, and of course, depression. Emotional intelligence is the necessary skill needed to stay calm in any stressful situation. By being aware of your emotions and regulating them in the way that is needed, you're able to mitigate your reactions by refraining from impulsive decisions. Before you respond to anything that you go through with immediate anxiety and negativity as your default reaction, think about the situation rationally. Is it really as bad as it seems? 90% of the time, things feel a lot worse than they are because of the way we choose to respond. By learning to respond without reacting, you're assessing the situation internally and acknowledging the way you feel, but on the outside, you try to maintain and calm and cool composure without giving away how you feel. This gets easier to do with emotional intelligence, which gives you the capacity to (even in your highly emotional state) understand the consequences of your actions.

❖ How To Master And Control Anger

You can hold a grudge for years because of your anger. You may know people you have not spoken to for a very long time because you still feel angry towards them, or maybe you are just supposed to. Some may find themselves having dangerous suicidal thoughts, perhaps even having tendencies of violence. These are the results of being unable to express anger appropriately, choosing instead to keep it buried inside.

Your anger can prevent you from living a meaningful, happy life. If you constantly find yourself feeling disgruntled, irritated, and frustrated more than you are happy, and even the smallest of instances can set you off, if you're verbally, emotionally (sometimes even physically) abusive towards others around you, then you may suffer from excessive anger. If you do, you may find that it spills over not just into your personal and professional life. If you have an anger problem, you need to learn now how to control it.

Anger is not only a problem when it's violent temper tantrums and shouting matches. Repressed anger can be just as much of a problem. This unexpressed anger works the same way as a volcano does. It bubbles and boils under the surface until one day, when something sets you off, all that repressed anger just comes shooting out with catastrophic consequences. Anger, which is not expressed or shown, is just as bad as anger that is evidently displayed. Either way, you spin it, anger is a big problem that can't be ignored. When the situation is as the one described above, anger is the first emotion that needs to be taken control of. This is also the case if you're dealing with someone who resorts to anger bursts whenever they open nether mouth.

Controlling anger is not about suppression. Suppression is not the goal. The goal here is to learn how to control that anger and understand why you are reacting the way you are. To learn how to respond better without overheating as your first immediate reaction. To be able to effectively handle situations that would have normally aggravated you without losing control. That is the goal of learning how to control your anger. For subjects affected by anger fits, denying their anger issues is one of the WORST things they could do, as it will not help them learn to control it. The more one denies his emotions and anger issues, the worst it will be for him when it comes to managing them. A more likely scenario is he finds himself feeling angrier and losing his temper even more because he feels helpless and unable to control the situation.

Mastering anger's emotions, like everything else, comes down to the right coping techniques and skills to get the situation under control. To effectively do that, you need to:

* **LOOK AT THE ROOT REASON**—Anger always stems from something. There is always a cause and a trigger. Your childhood, a traumatic experience, your role models growing up, your stress levels. All these things add up and could build anger problems. To begin learning how to control your anger, you must first explore and connect with the core reason anger is your first line of response and how you control it. Did you know that your anger is very often a response that is meant to cover up other feelings that you may have? That is why exploring the root reason is the only way to treat the problem at its core. What are those feelings? Jealousy? Embarrassment? Hurt? Shame? Insecurity? These are some of the reasons you need to think about. When the last time you asked yourself was: "Why am I REALLY angry?"

* **DISTRACT, DON'T REACT**—Anger is such a disruptive emotion. It causes a lot of hurt, pain, trauma, and worse, physical hurt at times. All common sense just seems to go out the window in the heat of the moment. Distracting instead of reacting is not always easy, but it does get better with practice. Instead of choosing to act on your emotions, deflect your attention elsewhere until you've forgotten about what it was that was threatening your temper. You need to distance yourself from your emotions for as long as it takes until you are properly distracted enough to forget what it was you were about to feel angry about.

* **THINK HAPPY THOUGHTS, DO HAPPY THINGS**—Peter Pan may have got it right when he said: "Think happy thoughts." People who struggle with anger issues have a lot of misery and unhappiness inside them. How can you learn to control your anger if you're still harboring all that negativity inside you? There's nothing better at getting rid of all those unhappy, miserable feelings than simply thinking about and doing something that makes you happy. Indulge in a passion or a hobby, and throw yourself into an activity that you love. A happier state of mind makes it easy to think with a clearer head, you don't get as worked up so easily anymore, and it becomes much easier to learn how to control your anger issues.

* **EMOTIONAL JOURNALING**—It may not be for everyone, but it can be very therapeutic when it comes to controlling your anger issues. One of the challenges when it comes to anger is that you're so overwhelmed with all sorts of emotions (anger, frustration, irritation) that it all comes out all at once. Many people tend to strike out or lash out in anger because they don't have the proper channels or outlets to release that anger. It gives you a safe and private place where you can express every feeling and emotion you have without the fear of being ridiculed or judged. Even better, it is possible the safest outlet for you to release your feelings of anger with repercussions without hurting anyone or yourself in the process.

Practice 4–steps Meditation – *Anger Management*

Meditation helps you control your emotions both in the moment of anger and in the long term. To meditate in the moment of anger, first remove yourself from the situation causing the anger.

(1) Take slow, deep breaths to bring down your elevated heart rate.

(2) Breathe deep enough that your belly extends on the "in" breath.

(3) Visualize a golden-white light filling your body as you breathe in.

(4) When you breathe out, visualize muddy or dark colors leaving your body.

(5) Once calm, think about your emotions.

(6) 6 Practice daily meditation.

(7) Decide how to deal with the situation that angered you.

❖ **How To Master And Control Anxiety**

Anxiety is another emotion that needs to be taken care of. It can easily be confused with and mistaken as fear; an easy way to distinguish between the two emotions would be to remember this rule of thumb: **Anxiety is less intense, but the effects are more prolonged, and a response related to anxiety-causing triggers.** On the other hand, fear is more of an immediate reaction to events or stimuli that are especially threatening. For many, anxiety is an all too familiar state of mind. Everyone experiences this to some degree throughout the various stages of our life. Most of the time, it is uncomfortable but still manageable. Others may deal with it more frequently, and when they do, anxiety becomes a nuisance, a hindrance, and sometimes feels like mental torture disrupting their daily routine when it culminates in a panic attack.

In our brain, there is one emotional part and a cognitive domain. The frontal lobe is where all our thoughts and the different sensations we experience come together. This also happens to be the cognitive part of the brain. The emotional part of the brain is where the amygdala lies. When we feel anxious, the emotional part of the brain starts to go into overdrive, overpowering the cognitive part, and that seeps into our consciousness. Anxiety has a way of creeping up on you, and you can't explain why. When anxiety is excessive, it can lead to a full-blown panic attack. For those who deal with anxiety and frequent panic attacks, their way of responding to anything the brain perceives as overwhelming can block their ability to function normally. When anxiety becomes a problem, our brain functions differently, such as failing to function or setting off irrational behaviors.

❖ How To Master And Control Depression

LEADING CAUSES OF DEPRESSION

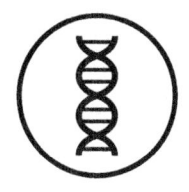

Biological causes such as hereditary presence of depression	Psychological causes negative parental influence	Socio-economic causes such as poverty and migration

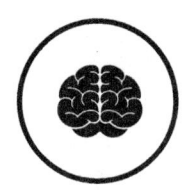

Negative experiences affect our brains in a much bigger way. When someone hurls hurtful words in your direction, it's not always easy to brush it off, and even harder to forget about it. Even if ten good things happened to you today, all it takes is **one** bad event to completely make you forget about the other ten. It's all you'll focus on for the rest of the day, and your mood takes a significant turn for the worst when it does. You could remember those encounters for days, weeks, years, maybe even throughout your lifetime. It's the same reason why those suffering from depression have a hard time pulling themselves out of that negative emotional cycle. Feeling down or miserable occasionally is not uncommon. It's the way we respond and cope with the events or situations that take place in our lives. Our emotions need an outlet.

Clinical depression is the one you need to worry about. There is a very big difference between feeling blue occasionally and being depressed. Feeling unhappy or sad every now and then is ok, as they are emotions that pass or get better with time. Depression does not. It is an intense emotion that lasts a lot longer. It impacts your ability to function in your daily routine, and you must take it seriously. The problem is that it's not always easy to tell when someone is going through depression. The changes in their mood and behavior could happen so gradually that it is barely noticeable; therefore, the signs are easy to miss. It is even harder if the person going through the emotion does not want to talk about how they feel. It is a condition that comes in several forms, some of which may require treatment or medication to treat the problem.

Yes, it may take a considerably long time and a lot of effort and help to overcome that hill, but when you do, things eventually start to feel like they are getting much better.

- Taking Each Day as It Comes—Give yourself a break and remember that some things take time. There's no magic cure or formula that will take your depression away overnight. The best recovery technique you can start with is to take things one day at a time.
- Find Your Reason When You Feel Like Quitting—Depression is a dangerous emotion because of the suicidal thoughts it can cause when it leads you down that dark path. As hard as it is, you need to find a reason to keep on putting one foot in front of the other. Even more so on the days when you feel like quitting and giving up entirely. Keep going because all we can do is take one step forward. Having a goal or something to fight for will help you

with this stage. It can be one reason, two, or several. It's only the overwhelming feelings you're experiencing that make it difficult to count your blessings. Let that be your reason.

- All You Need Is One—Tying in with the point above, all you need is one reason to be grateful each day to start taking steps toward conquering your depression once and for all. Use this reason as an anchor that leads you through the rest of the day. Repeat your reason throughout the day as a reminder that even in your darkest moments, there is at least one thing in your life you are still grateful for. Family, for example. Or the love of a supportive partner. Anything that gives you a reason to keep going. Focus on one to start and gradually work your way up as you start to feel better. Each time you feel your thoughts starting to get the best of you, return to your reason to be grateful today and concentrate on that until you feel better.

- This Is Not Forever—There is a light at the end of the tunnel. The unhappiness and misery will not last forever unless you allow them to. Sad times will come and go. Each time you feel overwhelmed with depression, remind yourself that this storm will pass. This darkness is not going to last forever, not when you keep fighting each day to see the light again.

- Exhibit Kindness—Especially to yourself. That you're unworthy and unlovable, if you're going to feel happy again, you need kindness as a start, especially toward yourself. Accept the way that you feel because your emotions are part of who you are. It's not wrong to feel the way you do, and you shouldn't beat yourself up over it. Judging yourself too harshly is a bad habit that must be broken for the sake of your mental and emotional well-being and happiness. Good or bad, emotions are part of who you are. Own them. Every single one, even the ones that make you anxious.

- Do Good for Others—Since depression can leave you with a lot of bad feelings and unhappy emotions, it's time to balance that out. One way to counter negative emotions is to do something good that lifts your spirits. Empower yourself by doing something good for someone else without expecting anything in return. If you can do something good for someone, do it. It will make their day better and put a smile on their face. Knowing that you've made a difference in someone's life will remind you that you're not as "useless" or "hopeless" as depression would have you believe. Focusing on doing well takes your mind away from the worries for a moment and reminds you that we are important and can make the difference.

Be Successful

As an empath, I've found that the most effective way to take care of yourself and to defend yourself from any attacks from outside, being a narcissist, an energy vampire, or a dark empath, is to reach that personal independence in whatever you want to achieve in your life. Do you want money? Make it. You want to build strong relationships in your life. Go ahead and plan it. Do you want to give and help others? Go out there and contribute as much as you can. Create your independence so that you can focus on discovering who you are.

SELF-DISCIPLINE, MENTAL TOUGHNESS AND RESPONSIBILITY

As an empath, one of the most precious skills you can learn to navigate through life-controlling where you're going, is self-discipline. But what is self-discipline?

- Self-discipline refers to self-control, which is the ability to avoid excessive unhealthy intake of anything that may lead to negative consequences.

- One of the central components of self-discipline is giving up immediate and instant satisfaction and pleasure to obtain some more significant gains or more satisfactory results, even if it requires effort and time.

The word self-discipline often causes some discomfort and resistance. It is due to wrong ideas, even if people feel unpleasant, difficult to achieve, and requires a lot of effort and sacrifice. Exercise and self-discipline can be fun, do not require strenuous effort, and have great benefits.

If you look around, you will find that although people's abilities are not very different, there are usually large differences in attitudes and results. Successful people succeed because they have a more positive attitude and a stronger mentality.

They created a series of strong routine thinking, which exudes naturally from their thoughts and feelings to their actions and behaviors. Even in the face of stress and pressure, these thinking habits will become second nature. This way of thinking enables them to take full advantage of opportunities and successfully meet the challenges they face. You are responsible for your mental preparation and for being armed with a focused, firm, and decisive attitude.

Find Your Purpose

Once you find your goal in life, everything starts to get easier because you understand why you do what you do. Being passionate about achieving your goals feeds your dreams and can give you clarity, which will make you confident in your everyday decisions. See how everything follows a perfectly logical cause-effect dynamic and once you are clear about your goals, all the pieces will start to fall into place.

Set and Achieve Your Goals and Milestones

To make your dream a reality, you are required to determine, choose and achieve a series of short-term goals to get you where you need to go. Once you select a goal, you will be more motivated to achieve it. Make a decision, hold yourself accountable for it, gather intention, and go. This focus will make you more determined and resolute as time goes by.

A positive attitude is everything

If you believe in yourself and believe that you can accomplish anything you want, you will have the confidence to deal with new challenges. Knowing exactly where you are going and why you will do it will help your confidence a lot because you don't need to second-guess yourself.

Keep in mind the firm idea that you will get there eventually. You have all the abilities that you need and more. Make optimism and positivity toward life a habit.

Accept The Challenges

If it were simple, everyone would do it, but the more difficult the challenge, the more people give up. Taking the easy path. Is always alluring. By accepting challenges and taking risks instead, you can create growth, and when it's time to reap results, you will jump ahead of those who stayed on the old, easy path. If you let yourself be paralyzed by fear, you will have all the time in the world for fine-combing and also making up your limits and boundaries that keep you from succeeding... Unless you accept setbacks on the road to realize your dreams, you will not achieve your goals.

Don't Give Up

Whatever you do, don't give up. Failure is very often on the path to success, and we can even say that it is an essential part of success. Stand back up. Learn better. Strike back. You must adopt a mentality that allows you to create opportunities from adversity and move on, no matter how difficult it is.

Outside Your Comfort Zone

Each of us has our personal "comfort zone," which is more than an actual place. It is a psychological/emotional/behavioral structure that defines our daily lives, where we have learned to survive. Being in a comfort zone means familiarity, safety, and security.

It describes the regular world in which we exist, makes us relatively comfortable and calm, and helps us remain emotionally stable and free from anxiety and worries. Creating a comfortable region is a healthy adaptation for most of our lives. However, when transition, growth, and transformation are needed, we must step out of our comfort zone.

It is also good to experience a little stress and anxiety occasionally. If all you do is wrap in a small cocoon and stay warm and comfortable, you may miss many things, such as new experiences, challenges, and risks. If approached in the right way, pain is a great asset in our lives. Pain is the signal we need to realize that evolution is possible.

If you cannot get out of your comfort zone, you may not encounter the difficulties that will force you to make changes and grow. Growing, learning, and evolution are what give meaning to our lives.

Your "real life" awaits you there. Your real life exists outside the bubble of your thoughts, feelings, and beliefs. As powerful as you may be inside, you have to use the potential of your inner power to thrive on the outside too. Your real life is the sum of all experiences, not just the experiences you are satisfied with. Challenging yourself will prompt you to dive into and utilize your storage of untapped knowledge and resources. Unless and until you venture out of the world you are familiar with, you can't know your purpose. Regardless of the outcome, taking risks is an experience of growth. Even if you made a mistake or didn't get it right the first time, you can use it in the future. If you learn to learn from experience, there is no such thing as "failure." Start to understand "failure" as "the first attempt to learn."

Don't settle for mediocrity to avoid getting out of your comfort zone; the price to pay is too high. Your challenges and risk experience are cumulative.

Whenever you try something new and allow yourself to open up to any experience that comes up, you learn and expand the scope of life skills and self-knowledge. When you do this, you will also expand the size of your comfort zone. Leaving your comfort zone will ultimately help you cope with changes and make better decisions. The turning points in life are all about change. You will move to another level every time you switch. These life changes will inevitably change you.

Walking into the unknown world seems like a jump into the dark. However, don't think about the "big picture" make small changes instead to break down the work you want or need to accomplish. Small changes accumulate, and each change is based on the last change. Try to make some small changes to get you out of the daily and familiar, where we don't have many emotional challenges. We all follow our long-established habits, but we also have the ability to create new ones. Change your daily work habits; try something that has never been done. You can start with little things: put your shoes on in a different place. Wake up 15 minutes earlier. Try to listen to that style of music that you could never stand. Carry out any type of creative project to drive your thoughts in new directions, add new ideas to your life, and open up to fresh experiences.

Why Failure Is the Key to Success

You can never find happiness if you do not evolve, and in order to evolve, pain is essential. Pain allows us to learn quickly from our mistakes. Touching a sharp object, falling, bumping into something, dropping something on foot; all these pain stimulators make children know not to do these things again in order not to experience pain again. Without pain, children would not learn from failure. Thanks to it, they will efficiently know how to not feel pain the next time they're around the same situations.

After entering adulthood and professional life, failure is often seen as a negative thing. If a company launches a new product, tries a new marketing plan, or tries a unique user experience on its website, chances are high that it won't be a success. So do we, and hence the fear of failing.

Failure Is a Functional to Succeeding

The best way to measure progress is the number of setbacks and "failures" encountered. If you have not failed, then you are not working hard enough. Failure is the hammer of the blacksmith, the sword he's creating is a success. If you want to be good at something, you must fail at least a few times. If you look back at all the great men in history, you will find that they have one thing in common. They failed greatly. Think of Thomas Edison. How many times he couldn't find a suitable filament for his bulb? Thousands. Henry Ford knew failure very well too. He said, "Failure is an opportunity to start again wisely." The precious element of failing is that when you start over, you're not starting from zero but from one step closer to your goal. And this is true also in relationships.

Treat Failure as a Tool

Those who are real "failures" cannot use failure as a tool. When you feel that sinking, desperate feeling called failure sinking in your heart, do not self-abate, but remind yourself to feel lucky. Now you can reallocate energy to the right external events. Identify the cause of failure and go make up for it.

When you feel you've hit bottom, ask yourself the following questions:

- What caused the failure?
- How much of it is in my sphere of influence?
- How can I manage what I can control to turn failure into success?
- What steps do I need to perform to go at it again?
- What should I do every day (routinely) to make sure that my next attempt is smarter?

You may want to take out a piece of paper and jot down a list. When you ask yourself each question, please be completely open and honest in your answers. Analyze them carefully and implement them right away—do not delay! Remember, failure is a chance, not a burden. Thank yourself and the setback for the opportunity to grow.

The Right Mindset to Defeat Procrastination

As an empath, I know that you have a long list of projects and tasks that need to be completed. You deal with everyone and then with your feelings about everyone, and you may have a list of things that need your attention. I also know how the items on the list may trouble you; sometimes, we feel overwhelmed that going through everything will never be possible. The truth is that we need a lot of self-discipline to get the job done.

And guess what: learning self-discipline is painful. But as we said, everything that is painful will bring change and happiness in the long run.

If you admit that you can improve your self-discipline and are determined to overcome the excuses your brain tends to create, I promise you will be ready to celebrate. Even achieving the minor milestones, we set for ourselves is beneficial and motivates us to continue working hard to achieve our goals.

Don't Punish Yourself for Success

Enjoy every little step that you make. If you've been able to express your feeling to that person, rejoice. If you have successfully helped someone, take credit for it. If you complete one of the items on your to-do list, resist the urge to add another project immediately.

If you carry into your daily tasks the self-blame that you may sometimes fall into, your enthusiasm could lead you to stress and burnout. Instead, reward yourself through good self-care. Read a book. Watch a movie. Sit in a garden and meditate. Go and see your loved ones. Go do your hair and think about what you have achieved so far.

Do everything you feel will regenerate you. The only thing I'll advise you not to do is doing nothing. Do not allow your brain to stall and enter that state that can leave space for your old, inefficient self to get back into play. Relax, but keep yourself busy. If anything, take a healthy nap. Doing physical exercises, hobbies, or just taking time out for a walk will help you clear your mind and refresh your next task.

Remember the 80/20 Rule

If you are not familiar with it, it is usually called the Pareto principle. According to this rule, 20% of what you do is responsible for 80% of the results you achieve. Once you know the values you stand for, and what you want to achieve for yourself, try to identify your 20%. Is it talking each day with five people? Is it writing in your journal your daily progression? Is it identifying the people that are damaging you? Or is it studying and perceiving the feelings of who's around you?

If you're after a business goal, know that 80% of your time will be dedicated to trivial tasks. The sooner you prune those out, the better you will reach your center and independence. Start tracking the time you spend to understand where your attention is going. After two to three days, you will know what you are doing and how long everything takes. Keep the essential parts and discard the rest, commission. Getting in the habit of doing this will revitalize your life.

Determining the Most Beneficial Habits

Although there is a subjective understanding of the word success, all people that have reached it have something in common. If you want to succeed, you should include these in your personality kit. Please note that the following traits are not innate. Even if you feel that you do not have some of these qualities, it is just a matter of practice and of making them part of your daily life.

The Desire and Motivation to Succeed

Here's a crucial principle: at every moment in life, you should have one or more goals you want to achieve. These wishes will keep you going and be your wake-up call when pain hits.

They work as checkpoints, which will lead to the ultimate goal of achieving what you need. If you feel that your desires are waning or your motivation is fading, try making some small changes to your goals, or better, find smaller goals that will help you reach the big one. Break down your long-term goals into smaller short goals that are easier and quicker to complete. Keep track of every step. Life is easy once you are able to deconstruct it into smaller bits.

Willingness to Change

People with the understanding that they are a work in progress are always ready for professional and personal growth. Acquiring new skills and knowledge will help you get the position you need to become the person you need to be. You should be open to knowledge that you may never have even known existed. Tasks that you've never considered. Obstacles are an excellent opportunity for you to grow. By managing newly discovered problems, learning new skills, or acquiring new knowledge, you can grow in whatever field you pursue. You will also grow as a person—you will learn to deal with new situations and stay calm under stress and pressure.

Adventurous and Disciplined Faith

An adventurous person is always looking for new and better opportunities. These often seem unsafe and uncertain. However, if you want to succeed, sometimes you need a leap of faith and dive into the unknown. Even if the odds are not by your side, this is not a reason to give up without trying. If you are prepared to fail, try, fail again, get back up and try until you have reached your goal, you'll see how the world will respond to your resilience.

Strict discipline is one essential characteristic of successful people. However, you want to put it, achieving success in any aspect of life is hard work, and there is no effective work without self-discipline, together with blind faith in the fact that you are a worthy person and life will give you not an ounce less of what you deserve.

Be Firm and Don't Give Up

A strong will paves the road to success. If you want to go down this road, you will inevitably have to make decisions. Some of them are easy, while others will not. Sometimes you will be right, some other times, you will be massively wrong. But they all will be necessary. When difficult times come, our instinct usually tells us to run to avoid unpleasant situations. Managing this instinct is what will distinguish who will grab ahold of the opportunities of life and those who won't.

Think Positive and Find Your Focus

Because empaths are highly sensitive people, the high-intensity stimuli of the world can lead them to fall into periods of depression. As I said before, this can be very dangerous and will only make any situation they can be into worse. So, I can't stress enough the importance of positive thinking.

Remember this: staying positive and optimistic will attract reasons to be positive and optimistic.

Positive thinking can be achieved through various effective methods, and here are some methods to help you get started and help you train your brain to think positively.

Focus on Good Things

Challenging situations and obstacles are a piece of life. And a very useful one!

When something good happens in your life, no matter how small or insignificant you may think it is, you should focus on it. When something bad happens, focus on the good things, memories, and people life has gifted to you. Our brain cannot tell the difference between reality and something vividly imagined. So, consider the power you have upon your brain: you can distract it, and misdirect it into focusing on something better than the actual event you're living, with the corresponding feeling going with it.

One of the most useful pieces of advice I could give you is to turn your television set off. Television is paid to entertain you. Entertainment uses conflict as a device to keep your interest high. Conflict hurts your brain and your mood (many researches have been done on the topic, and all point to the same result: cognition is embodied). The same can be said of social media, with the pejorative addition of algorithm customization, which makes it even more dangerous.

Focus instead on good vibes; be attracted to what is beautiful in the world. Always look at the bright side, and you will be brighter yourself.

Practice Gratitude

Taking each chance, we have to be grateful has proved that it can reduce stress, improve self-esteem and enhance adaptability even in tough times. The most successful people are grateful. Think about friends, moments, or things that can bring you some comfort or happiness, and attempt to express your gratitude at least once a day, maybe as you meditate. Being grateful will improve your optimism and happiness. How about writing a "Thank you diary" every day or writing down a list of things you are grateful for when encountering difficulties? You might want to thank a colleague for helping with a project, a loved one for washing the dishes or thank your dog for their unconditional love. Gratitude can also be a weapon to catch a person hurting you off guard.

Spend Time with Positive People

It is said you are the result of the five people that are closest to you. Whether they are positive or negative, they are contagious. People you spend time with will influence the way you see life, your attitude toward it and, most importantly, will constitute the standards you will expect and will obtain from life. Consider who is around you. Are they depressed? Are they always angry? Are they full of energy? Are they constantly empowering you? If they're not, consider knowing new, more empowering individuals. Just by doing this, you can improve your life.

Engage in Active Self-Talk

We are often the harshest individual in judging ourselves. When you repeat this over time, it may form negative autosuggestion and disempowering opinions about yourself, and once it is sedimented in your sense of identity, it is difficult to shake off. To prevent this, you need to pay attention to the voice in your head and respond with positive self-talk. Research shows that even small changes in the way you talk to yourself can affect your ability to regulate your feelings, thoughts, and behaviors under pressure. An example of positive self-talk could be, instead of saying, "I messed up," say, "I will try again in another way." Be always open to possibilities and opportunities, and shut that negative voice with constructive logic.

Deal with Your Negative Areas

Take a close look at all aspects of your life and identify areas most likely to be negative. Uncertain? Ask a trusted friend or colleague. They have the opportunity to provide some insight. A colleague may notice that you tend to be negative at work. Your spouse may notice that you become significantly negative while driving—process one area at a time. Create a ritual that allows you to start with exciting and positive things every day. Here are some ideas:

- Tell yourself that this will be a good day, or use any other affirmation that you see fit.

- Listen to happy and positive songs or playlists.

- Share some positive attitudes by praising or doing something good for someone.

Resist Instant Gratification

You try to lose weight, you go visit your mom and she has prepared your favorite cake. What do you do? If you succumb and fill your plate with candies, this may derail your diet, but you will get immediate satisfaction. If you can resist and spend an evening eating salad and chewing carrot sticks, and then repeat it, you may get a greater return—reduce that excess weight and be able to wear your favorite jeans. This ability to resist temptation and adhere to our goals is often referred to as willpower or self-control.

Delayed gratification is a core part of this behavior. We postponed the fulfillment of our present desires so that we could get better things in the future.

Choosing long-term rewards for instant gratification is a significant challenge in many areas of life that can pay off. From avoiding a piece of chocolate cake when we try to lose weight to staying at home to study rather than going to parties with friends, the capacity to delay gratification can be the difference between reaching our goals or not. Here are some tips to achieve it:

1. **Know your values**. When you know what is essential to you, you can make choices to make yourself happy and successful.

2. **Know what you want to achieve**. Make sure you have clearly defined goals. What do you want to achieve? A clear conclusion of what you want to accomplish in the long term can help you choose delayed gratification to achieve your ultimate goal.

3. **Make a plan**. When you understand your values and know the goals you want to achieve, developing a plan to help you achieve your goals can remind you of the choices, you need to make in the process and strengthen delayed gratification.

4. **Priority**. Being able to prioritize what is essential to you and what you want to achieve can help you choose a time to delay gratification.

Set Objective and Attainable Goals

VISUALIZATION: PROBLEM SOLVING AND GOAL SETTING

Visualization is a simple technique that can be used to create strong psychological impressions of future events. Taking full advantage of the visualization function, you can practice for the event in advance to prepare for the event. By visualizing success, you can build the confidence needed to perform well. For example, suppose you have an essential job interview next week. You are already nervous; you're worried that the answers to the interviewer's questions will be poor, you will speak awkwardly about your past results and forget the recommendation letter. Or you may take a deep breath and train yourself during the week by visualizing the interview going exactly as it should: you are completely in control of your voice and emotions, and you reply quick-wittedly to every question the interviewers send your way. Rehearse the scene twice a day, and see the result.

VISUALIZATION HAS THE FOLLOWING ADVANTAGES:

- ★ **Visualizing the results, you want will increase your confidence.** "Seeing" your success can help you believe that it can and will happen.

- ★ **Visualization can help you "practice" success.** When you imagine that every step of an event or activity is going well, you can prepare to take these steps in real life.

- ★ **Anyone can benefit from visualization.** You don't need to be a life coach or personal development expert to use visualization to achieve your goals. You just do it.

To start visualizing your goals, these are the steps:

Decide What You Want

What do you want to focus on? Choose a dream or goal and start to imagine it. For example, visualize the successful results of the presentation to be performed next week.

Describe The Scene

Start to imagine the exact scene. Don't be vague or unclear—the more specific you are, the more details you can imagine, the better the visualization. Imagine the scene as being present. What are you wearing? Who is in the room with you? Make sure to use all senses in the visualization exercises. Sight, sound, taste, smell, touch- all of these must be included so that you can truly bring your vision to life. In our example, visualize yourself standing in front of the group. Picture the face of each team member and the clothes each person is wearing. Listen to the sound of paper being moved around, the smell of fresh coffee, the sight of sunlight shining through the office windows. Imagine yourself setting up your notes confidently and starting your speech.

Imagine Every Step Towards a Successful Conclusion

What must you do to ensure a successful demonstration? Identify each step that must be taken to achieve the goal. And start describing each step as part of the visualization exercise. For example, your presentation will start with an introduction. Therefore, imagine yourself explaining the presentation's main thesis to the group and what they will get from it. Visualize the talking points you will use and what each slide will say. Imagine your gestures and imagine looking at everyone when you speak. Imagine they understand everything you say and agree with every word.

Go through the whole presentation in your mind, focusing on each step and noticing how you feel. Remember, always concentrate on what you want, not what you don't need. You want to relax and be confident, not nervous or forgetful. Therefore, focus on positive emotions and avoid negative ones.

Daily Visualization

You want to perform a whole visualization at least one time a day until the actual day comes. It's essential to be consistent because regular visualization can make your brain believe that what you imagine is real. The more you visualize events, the stronger your vision, and the more likely you will get what you want. Why? Because you are convincing your nervous system that giving presentations, for example, is something you normally do. Daily visualization is like training for a marathon or completing a golf swing. The more you prepare, the more familiar your body (or mind) will become with these specific "actions." You are training your mind to achieve successful results. The great thing about visualization is that you can do this anywhere: on the train to and from get off work, before going to bed at night, or while drinking coffee in the morning.

Can an Empath Be Extroverted?

When an empath is also an extrovert, we find a powerful combination in which the person has an immense quantity of fuel to connect with others. Being an Extroverted Empath is not necessarily more difficult than being an Introverted Empath. Still, there are some aspects that extroverts should keep in mind while navigating social interactions, or they could end up feeling drained or depleted.

Extroverts tend to be more tuned into their emotions and react more quickly to certain situations. An Empath is easily tired by the pace of constant emotion and chatter that tends to run through an Extroverted Empath's mind. Even though Extroverted Empaths' minds can run wild, they can use their intuitive ability to connect with others more effectively in a calm manner. When they conquer the ability to stay calm and focused, the empath can communicate fully and efficiently with another person better than a non-empath person would.

The Extroverted Empath's ability to stay calm in the face of constant emotion is a powerful tool that they can use to connect with others on a deeper level. The feeling of these kinds of empaths will often be visible from the outside, as they will not always be able to contain the emotional storm within them. When their emotions are displayed, it is also easier for others to connect with them because they look more open and honest. When Extroverted Empath loses their cool, they tend to lose their voice while communicating.

If you are an Extroverted Empath, by using your ability to empathize, you can improve your ability to listen. An Empath's natural tendency is to want to jump in and talk about how they would feel in that situation. Instead, we can be non-judgmental listeners that can provide a calming presence with empathy. We can open ourselves up to others without overwhelming them with our feelings. The ability to shut off your thoughts and accept others is an extremely powerful tool for understanding. It allows the Empath to feel what others are really feeling.

When we listen to someone who has just had negative energy aimed at them, we can use empathy to understand how they feel and give them space if needed. Instead of filling the silence with our thoughts, we can focus on letting them talk and taking in everything they have to say. The most powerful tool an Extroverted Empath has is the power of listening. Using this skill, you can create a sense of acceptance and understanding in your interactions with others.

If you're feeling someone's emotions too strongly, it is ok and also helpful to express your feelings. By using the ability to empathize with others, you can speak about your own emotions and theirs. You are deeply able to provide a sense of reassurance and validation that will allow them to talk about their issues without overloading them with our emotions.

Always Learn New Skills!

If you are at the point where you need to heal from an abusive relationship, hobbies are a wonderful way to support your healing journey. They are great for distracting you from what you have experienced, offering you a boost of confidence by giving you a sense of understanding and knowledge over something you enjoy, at the same time connecting you with other people who share the same passion, and support you in networking and promoting a sense of joy within you. There are many positive benefits to having a hobby.

The key when healing from an abusive relationship that encouraged self-isolation is to choose a hobby that is going to push you in meeting other people. If you enjoy something that tends to be more solitary, such as reading, consider joining a book club that would allow you to get together with others and begin socializing in a normal setting again.

You could have an old hobby that you abandoned or it can be a new one, there are plenty of options. This is a great time to practice listening to your inner desires and needs, and doing something you love. Choosing something that you are interested in and that will bring you some joy is a wonderful way to remind yourself that you are worthy of having happiness in your life and that happiness is something you deserve to experience. This could include playing a musical instrument you have always wanted to learn, or perhaps taking up a new sport, or maybe learning to speak a new language. This is a great way to practice self-love and begin adding things back into your life that will help your evolution. It is also a great way to open yourself up to new opportunities.

In the beginning, focus on picking something that will be more manageable for you. Attempting to do too much at once or trying to get right back to where you were before the abusive relationship can be overwhelming and intimidating. When you realize that you are not the same person you were before the relationship and that your ability to do things the way you once did has changed, you may end up feeling uncomfortable. Starting off smaller and slower can support you in easing back into being a person with confidence, high self-esteem, and self-respect. Set manageable and reasonable goals for yourself and celebrate each success every time you achieve a result in your new hobby. This will make your healing journey much easier.

The Therapy Option

Therapy is something that would be beneficial to nearly everyone, regardless of the history of trauma. For someone who has survived narcissism, therapy is essential. Through therapy, you will learn to identify why you were a target for a narcissist, how to cope with whatever trauma led you to be an easy target and how to cope with all of the feelings surrounding your relationship with the narcissist.

Cognitive-behavioral therapy can be especially useful in restructuring your thoughts to become less vulnerable to the narcissist's clutches. If you are having trouble locating a therapist that would be good for you, you can speak to your primary care doctor and discuss what you have gone through and how you are feeling. Your doctor can provide referrals to licensed therapists in your area in a field of therapy that the doctor thinks may be beneficial.

Engage in Self-Care

After spending so long caring for the narcissist, caring for yourself can seem unnatural, but it is essential to healing. You are worthy of care, and without that, you will inevitably burn out. By relaxing and doing something you love, you will begin to feel more like your old self.

Take this one step further: make time daily to work on something about yourself that you wish to get better at, such as exercising more, eating healthier meals, or studying something you have always wanted to learn. Go back to school for a degree if you do not have one or do anything that will help better yourself. You likely spent time being convinced that you were incapable of thriving without the narcissist around, and it is time to prove to yourself that the narcissist was wrong.

Affirmations

Affirmations are a common technique used in CBT to help change a person's negative core beliefs into something more positive. They are often meant to reverse negative beliefs and strengthen and ground yourself in moments of weakness or when you feel yourself slipping back into your old ways. By creating a small arsenal of affirmations related to your healing from narcissistic abuse, you will be able to keep your mental clarity and focus on reversing the damage the narcissist has inflicted.

Affirmations can be almost anything, so long as they meet three key criteria: They must be positive, they must be about yourself and they must be present tense. By keeping your affirmation positive, you keep your mind rooted in positivity and slowly teach your mind to think in positives such as, "I need more practice," as opposed to, "I am no good at this." There is a huge difference in attitude between the two, and the positive thought lends itself more to productive behaviors, whereas the negative thought is very discouraging. They must be about yourself because ultimately, you only have control over yourself. You cannot influence other people's thoughts or feelings, and therefore, you cannot be entirely sure without a doubt that your affirmation is accurate if it involves someone else's mindset because you will never truly be privy to someone else's mind. Lastly, the affirmation in the present tense means it is true and effective at that particular moment.

For a victim of narcissistic abuse, an example of an affirmation could be, "I trust my perception of the world around me." As narcissists love to Gaslight to disarm their victims, reminding yourself that your perceptions are accurate helps assuage any self-doubt that may begin to creep up, especially in situations the narcissist in your life used to manipulate. Another affirmation could be, "I am worthy of respect and love." Narcissists break down your spirit and convince you that you are not worthy of either, usually because they are incapable of genuinely respecting and loving other people.

Be Gentle and Patient with Yourself

Remember, you are healing some major wounds inflicted by someone you trusted. This is a long process, and it is pretty typical to experience setbacks. Maybe you decided you missed the narcissist so much you contacted him despite knowing better, and you feel like all of the healing you have been doing has been undone in an instant. You feel like you are right back down in the trenches and ashamed and frustrated that you erased the progress.

Instead of seeing the progress as gone forever, remind yourself that the progress was not erased; grieving comes and goes. Grieving for your loved one or the relationship you should have had will not go away instantaneously; in fact, it may never completely go away, but it does become easier to live with over time. Healing from a narcissist is a lot like losing someone you love deeply; the person you thought you knew died with the narcissist's mask slipping, and it is normal to grieve it. Instead of focusing on how you messed up, instead, look back and see how far you have come since the beginning; you recognize the narcissist for what he is and can understand and identify the signs and tactics used against you for the duration of the relationship. While you may slip up from time to time, you are only human. You are not expected to be perfect. After you inevitably fall, pick yourself up, dust yourself off and keep going. With perseverance, you can, and you will heal from this.

Sustaining Your Relationship Through *the Gift of Empathy*

Bad relationships, however, can have a way of working out after all. They need effort, they need pain, and they need joy. In today's fast-paced world, relationships are complex and multifaceted, making things difficult to keep up. You need to know when it's time to walk away and when it's possible to come to a mutual understanding. Empathy is a strong instrument for restoring fractured relationships. When you are dealing with your partner, kindness is always the key you utilize to find your way out. But it's a long-term journey that requires effort and a lot of commitment.

The Real Secret to a Happy Relationship

You wouldn't have to use a certain formula of sorcery or venture through the depths of a wonderland in psychology to discover the key to a happier relationship. Our partnerships are based on mutual information and common convictions and experiences. In keeping with this rationale, despite life's struggles and adversities, our shared sense of empathy and compassion allows us to transcend challenges and remain connected.

It's normal to feel empathy towards another person, which involves putting oneself in their shoes and making the conscious effort to see things from their point of view. This extends beyond believing what they mean on a shallow basis to seeking to consciously understand the feelings to perceptions of the other person.

The love and empathy that we can have towards our spouses and partners go well beyond simple sympathy—which is merely meaning, "Yeah, I see your struggle"—to be willing to understand and respond to their suffering, joy, and also their crushing sorrow.

How to Re-Establish Empathy and Sustain Your Relationship

Although your relationship might have hit some major stumbling blocks, often times just by focusing on compassion and focusing on one another, you can find your way back to one another again. You can find your way back to a common ground if you allow yourself to reconnect on some basic levels. Such basic strategies are some of the strongest approaches in the cycle to reconnect to the sense of shared trust, awareness, and sustainability.

1. Listen with Intention

Learning how to build empathy for your partner will be the first step in learning how to listen with purpose. We get drawn in far too much and bogged down with the specifics of our daily suffering. Activated tunnel vision, we lose sight of our partner's desires and get distracted by our point of view and perspective. As we start listening—and doing so intentionally—to our partners, we find various pieces of them that we have never realized were there.

Establish a new communication channel for your partner, and do so openly and sincerely. Ask them questions and then listen carefully when answering them. Absorb and engage with what they say by questioning them and digging deeper into their point. Let go of the null mindset. Do not form answers before you try to say what they want to say in full. Repeat this daily until it transforms into a second habit and no one feels they're still trying to get their point across.

Rebuild and reconnect when possible. You achieve this by creating reliable contact modes daily, which will also contribute to the future you work together to build.

2. Communicate Kindly

Nevertheless, relationships are emotional, as are good and bad emotions. When a person crosses a line or makes us feel unwanted—we may find ourselves lashing out and breaking rules that we will normally never breach in our regular state of mind. That's why compassion needs to be expressed in talking and understanding again and why it's necessary to apply that to other facets of our lives.

Practice good contact with your companion (even though you're angry), and evoke it intentionally. Focus on integrity and always consider their reasons before reacting or allowing your emotions. Find an agreement about the situation you're discussing about. Why do you need to talk? Which language do you want them to use? Are you willing to listen to each other? There are essential criteria to decide, which will help you manage the interaction.

Gentle reactions to negative behavior, in return, will encourage kind reactions. Instead of setting up the flames and pushing one another further down, you can start constructing the connections you need by preferring to be friendly rather than mean when things get rough. It doesn't have to be hard to share something or a common understanding, even if you do not agree.

3. Show Your Appreciation

Sometimes, issues stagnate after you have been in a relationship for a long time. The relationship gets lost under all the many tiny pieces of experience that go together to build a life. We go on autopilot when we get stuck in a rut and often fail to give our partners the attention and appreciation they deserve (and need) in that room. If you want to be understood again, you can start by expressing some appreciation.

Thank them for their time and effort, and make it clear that you desire to reciprocate with little gestures of affection or understanding. We're not simply expressing gratitude through words. It is also something that we give through our deeds. This is the extreme effort you can try when dealing with someone who can still understand and find love back. It doesn't always work, but sometimes, it's worth it.

Conclusion

Thank you for making it through to the end. I hope that you've found this book to be helpful. Hopefully, you have learned something about yourself or how to deal with an empath.

Empaths are incredible human beings and need people that are able to understand their marvelous gifts. There can be no greater freedom than the ability to be who you are with no reservations. Empaths are given so many unique tools, from birth, above all, the ability to better their own lives and the lives of those close to them. It can be difficult to overcome the emotional barriers that come with such abilities, but I hope this book succeeded in helping readers with that. It is never too late to learn, heal, and get better. Growth is ageless. It doesn't matter how old or young you are, all that matters is that you are committed to exploring your gifts and empowering yourself. The only thing that can truly hold you back from living your best life and making the most of your gifts, is you. When you accept yourself and acknowledge your true nature, everyone else will find it impossible to resist your charms. Confidence and belief in your abilities will take you from being a hesitant empath to a powerhouse. The gifts you possess as an empath are abilities that you can use to make a difference in the world and touch other people's lives. Ultimately, an empath is a natural healer, nurturer, and protector. These are all qualities that the world sorely needs at this point. Let your compassion, creativity, and enthusiasm for life transform you and the people connected to you. Now that you have enhanced your knowledge of what it means to be an empath and how to use your abilities and manage challenges and challenging people, the next step is to start practicing the techniques and strategies outlined in this book. Start realizing the gifts that come from your empathic powers. You are the author of your own destiny. Watch yourself transform into the image of the person that you have always wanted to be.

★ *Good luck on your journey,* ★

Michelle

Make a difference in 60 seconds!
One last thing: we'd love to hear your thoughts on this book!

As a small publishing house, your support is invaluable to us. Your feedback can significantly impact everyone involved in bringing this book to life. Sharing how this book has benefited you can make a big difference.

I am sure you can imagine how difficult it is for an independent book to collect reviews. Yet, that's one of those little things that are crucial for the survival of a small publishing reality.

If this book has provided you with valuable insights, or knowledge that you've found valuable, your opinion truly matters to us. It's more than just a review; it's a vital support to everyone involved in bringing this book to life.

We take every piece of feedback to heart—in fact, we read every review personally. That is why we would be infinitely grateful if you could spare 60 seconds of your time and leave your genuine opinion.

Use this *LINK* (https://t.ly/6244M) or scan the QR code to leave a quick review on Amazon in less than a minute.

For feedback, constructive criticism, questions about the book's content, or request to delve deeper into the book's topics, you can reach out to us at phantapub@gmail.com

Sharing your experience can illuminate the path for future readers and guides us on our journey to create impactful work.

Thank you for your support!

If you enjoyed this book…
feel free to also check out on Amazon

Printed in Great Britain
by Amazon